D1643033

ITStarterSeries

presents

Programming

Computer Programming for Beginners: Learn the Basics of HTML5, JavaScript & CSS

By: Joseph Connor

4th Edition (2017)

ABOUT MJG PUBLISHING

MJG Publishing presents the IT Starter Series. We are an independent publisher focusing on non-fiction books. Our eBooks and paperback books are targeting to help individuals to upgrade their careers & lifestyle. Learn new skills & abilities. Find the job of your dreams or create your own freelancing opportunity!

CONTACT:

Visit our website: www.itstarterseries.com
Email us: marco@mjgpublishing.com

Follow our Social Media:
Facebook: https://www.facebook.com/mjgpublishing/
Twitter: https://twitter.com/MJG_Publishing
Instagram: https://www.instagram.com/mjgpublishing/

Feel free to contact us at any time and I'll personally reply to you.

Marco, Exclusive Publisher

MJG Publishing on behalf of Joseph Connor.

Free Video Course: Introduction to JavaScript, SQL & C++

Get access to a free video course covering the basics of JavaScript, Sql, & C++. Those computer programming languages is what you need to get a high paying job or to upgrade your career!

Click the below image or link to get immediate access:

Click this link: **http://www.itstarterseries.com/free-programming-course** **NOW** and get immediate access to your free video series!

Happy coding,
Marco

WANT TO LEARN MORE ABOUT PROGRAMMING?

Check out the other books by Joseph Connor:

<u>Newest release (2017): Programming: Computer Programming For Beginners: Learn the Basics of SQL</u>

C#: Computer Programming for Beginners: Learn the Basics of C Sharp Programming – 3rd Edition (2017)

Python: The Definitive Guide to Learning Python Programming for Beginners

Hacking: Hacking for Beginners - Computer Virus, Cracking, Malware, IT Security

The Amazon Bestseller: Programming: Computer Programming for Beginners: Learn the Basics of Java, SQL & C++ - 4. Edition (2017)

Table of Contents

Free Video Course: Introduction to JavaScript, SQL & C++

Welcome to the journey into the world of programming. Hi, I'm Marco from MJG Publishing, I wanted to thank you for supporting this book.

You're going to learn the 3 most in-demand programming languages with step-by-step real examples: JavaScript, SQL and C++.

If you study only ONE of those, you can have a good career in programming. Study all three of these and you will be highly thought of and in demand.

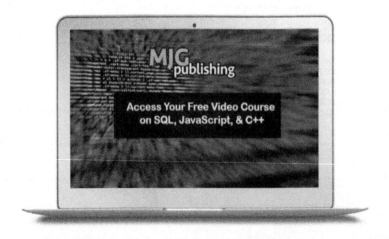

Click this link: **http://www.itstarterseries.com/free-programming-course** **NOW** and get immediate access to your free video series!

Find out on real examples which language suits you best and get access to our free BONUS. Receive access to code examples, learn about how to set up the different environments that you can use for programming and receive a step-by-step programming tutorial that you can put immediately into action at home.

Happy coding,
Marco

INTRODUCTION

The Internet is everywhere. In fact, you used the Internet to purchase this book. This was, of course, made possible by web development, the same thing you will be gaining an idea of in this book. The world of programming is vast, and web programming is just one of its sections, albeit a big one.

Web programming or, as it is more commonly known, web development, is the development of web applications. A web application can be something as simple as a web page, a social networking site or even a fully-fledged game. Like all kinds of programming, web development has its own programming languages that are used for developing those applications.

There are quite a few web development languages in use today. However, three of the most popular ones are HTML, JavaScript and CSS. Knowing these languages can give you a strong base which you can improve upon to become a fully-fledged web developer.

However, learning these programming languages can be a daunting task for someone who does not have prior programming experience and exposure. So, the key is to get a firm grasp of the basic fundamentals of the language. One should take things slowly rather than aiming at creating fancy scripts in the beginning. For beginners, the terminology used in the programming may become confusing sometimes. Terms such as "objects," "variables" and "elements" have a specific meaning in programming. Therefore, it becomes imperative to learn and use these terms.

In this book, you will be learning the basics of these three languages. You will understand the various fundamentals of each language such as the structure of the language and programming concepts. You will learn the syntax of each language along with the different kinds of functions. A "hello world" example has also been provided to help you understand the language at work. Apart from that, we have included some useful tips and tricks for these languages along with frequently asked questions on them. In short, you will be familiarized with all the things you need to know before taking up that language for coding in.

Let us now start learning HTML, CSS, and JavaScript.

CHAPTER 1
INTRODUCTION TO WEB
DEVELOPMENT

Websites are created for different purposes depending on the target audience. Some are made for selling products and some are just for providing information. Web development tools provide companies with a platform to create their web presence. Websites give them visibility with a wider audience. To develop a site in accordance with their requirements, businesses hire developers. Developing a website can include anything from simple programming to network security, adding content or web server configuration.

Programming involves a set of instructions that are written in a computer language or codes. A developer needs to have a thorough knowledge of the programming languages. Before you start learning how to program in different languages used on the web, it is essential to have an understanding of web development in general.

This will help you understand what you can expect from this field.

What is Web Development?

Web development can be broadly defined as the development of websites and web applications that will be hosted on the Internet or the intranet. In reality, web development is used as an umbrella term for a collection of activities such as web design, client-side coding, server-side scripting, network security configuration and other tasks.

Web development involves usage of scripting languages both at the client's site and at the server end. It ranges from creating plain text pages to complex applications. The web development hierarchy includes client side coding, server side coding and database technology.

More specifically, web development can be said to be web programming. This involves the creation of the code for making a web application or website. With it, you can create a simple web page to a massive social networking site such as Facebook or an e-Commerce portal like Amazon.

Web Development Process

Before you start building a website, the first and foremost thing is that you must understand what information or message you are trying to pass on to your viewers or customers. What is it that they are expecting to see in terms of the content? How can you make the content user-friendly and easy to navigate? Once all the front end design aspects are clear, one must start working on the backend of the website, which would include how to host, what architecture to use, what is the expected traffic load on the website and how can you setup an infrastructure to ensure that the overall built of the website is robust. Finally, one must ensure that the website can be opened on various types of browsers or devices like smart phones, tablets etc. and is easily searchable through search engines.

There are a number of steps involved in the web development process but, broadly, these can be classified into five phases.

1. Discovery- The first step in developing a website is to understand the requirements of the business which include the purpose of creating the site, target audience and the content of the site.

2. Definition- The information gathered in step one has to be compiled together to define a site map or plan for the website. It involves the creation of an easy to use navigational system or user interface.

3. Design- This step involves crafting a user experience. The visual appeal of the site depends on the template you choose and it should always be done keeping in mind the target audience. For example, a website targeting teenagers will have different elements to a website for a financial institution.

4. Development- In this step, the final design is implemented to create an actual functional site. Content management system and programming codes are used to develop the site.

5. Deployment- The complete functionality of the website is tested and once the business is satisfied with the final product the web site files are uploaded to the client's server.

Aspects of Web development

Web development can be broadly classified into two separate sections. They are front-end development and back-end development. In order to have a fully functional website, both of these processes need to go hand in hand.

Front-end Development: Also known as client-side coding, in this development, you will be creating what the user is going to see when a web application is loaded. This includes the design and the content along with how the user is going to interact with it. For front-end development, you need to use HTML, JavaScript and CSS.

HTML is the code used for turning text into a web page. All web pages are written in HTML, and this language is also pivotal for all web applications. CSS is used to set the style rules, and it determines how a web page will appear. JavaScript is used to adding functionality to web pages and make them more interactive.

Backend Development: This is also referred to as server-side coding. It determines what is happening in the server of the web page. In other words, the user does not get to see this activity, but it can affect the website. A common activity in backend development is the creation of a database for the generation of the front-end.

A variety of coding languages and frameworks are used in backend development. PHP, ASP.NET, Ruby on Rails, Python, Node.js and Java are some of them.

Pros and cons of using Programming languages

Programming languages are used to create programs for building a website or a web application. Most of the programming languages are easy to learn. They help you in adding dynamic and interactive activities to the web page. Complex tasks can be performed in relatively fewer steps.

You also get:

• Wonderful job satisfaction and the ability to use your mind and to put your creativity to the test

• To determine your own destiny in terms of your career. No longer will you find it difficult to get a good programming job. Or, if you prefer, you can go down the route of developing and marketing your very own software

- Decent pay – jobs for computer programmers start at around $60,000 and, in many cases, you can earn a whole lot more

- Better options for a career – learning how to program a computer can help you to move on to other jobs in technology

The downside of a programming language is that bugs while coding can be annoying and difficult to resolve sometimes. A web developer needs to know the syntax of a programming language like the back of their hand. Hence, a lot of hard work and a good memory are essentials. Moreover, one needs to build upon the speed for programming otherwise it is a very time-consuming activity.

Other downsides to learning how to program computers include:

- It's fast paced. If you are not comfortable with learning new information at a quick pace and competently then it may not be for you.

- You need to read quite a few books each year just to keep up with the latest computer upgrades and new technologies, as well as changes in programming guidelines.

- Computer programming is very much technology driven and if this is not something close to your heart, you might find yourself becoming unhappy with learning it

- It could cause health issues as you will be spending a good deal of time sitting down, typing, staring at a screen. You could suffer from pain in your eyes, wrists and lower back.

Why Learn Web Development?

Of course, the most common reason to start learning web development is to become a web developer yourself. You will be able to create web pages and websites for people to view over the Internet. However, that is not the only reason to learn web development. There are many reasons and we have listed a few of them:

1. One of the features of web development is that it is comparatively easy to learn. In fact, many programmers claim that web development is an excellent choice for those who wish to start learning to program. If you are interested in becoming a programmer, web development can provide you with a foundation in which to do so.

2. Learning web development can give you good job prospects. Businesses want to make an effective presence and, for that, they are under pressure to offer high-quality websites with e-commerce and communication capabilities. Hence more and more companies look out for web developers who can deliver the best.

3. As a web developer, you get an opportunity to create new cool things. You just need to have a laptop and an Internet connection with knowledge of programming language you can create with your imagination.

4. Web development is not about the web anymore. When companies think about creating websites today, they also think about social media and mobile technology. There is a surge in usage of smart phones, Internet TV, tablets and many other devices hence the developer needs to take into account all these. This expands the reach of developers.

5. Web development is quite flexible and has a lot of facets such as the front end, back end, content management systems, e-commerce, mobile web and more. This gives professionals a wide range of opportunities and at the same time, new tools are making the process of enhancing the skills much easier.

Now that you know what web development is about, let's get started with the actual languages of HTML, CSS, and JavaScript.

CHAPTER 2
LEARNING HTML5: THE LANGUAGE OF THE WEB

HTML is the core of the web. It is a standard that has become accepted by everyone. As such, understanding it will be the key to developing web pages and web applications.

Nearly all computer applications that read and write files make use of a special file format. For example, the Notepad application in Windows can understand and use '.txt.' files. These files will contain all the instructions on how the document should be displayed when opened along with the contents of that document and other data. HTML functions in a similar manner. This language describes the content of a web document.

Unlike other programming languages, like C++, HTML5 has very simple core concepts. The reason why beginners find it so difficult to learn has little to do with its complexity and more to do with the jargon and the acronyms that surround it, not to mention, in some cases, just bad writing.

Most people see the computer as logical and that isn't wrong – if you are another computer. The problem is that human and computer logic are two completely different things and those who do understand computer logic are somewhat different to the rest. It is this difference that makes these people good at working with computers but not so good at explaining them in a human logic manner. I hope that what I am about to explain is clear to you and is written in a language that you can understand and put to effective use.

What is HTML?

HTML is an abbreviation for Hyper Text Markup Language. It is the language used to create web pages. In fact, HTML is a cornerstone technology of the modern Internet, the language that dominates the World Wide Web. In fact, we can attribute a very large part of the Web to HTML and, with its creation and with the web browsers that can interpret it, anyone who has a computer and a phone line or fiber optic wire to their house, can surf the web and find all sorts of interesting stuff. Apart from web pages, it is used for creating user interfaces for the web and mobile applications.

It consists of a set of codes or markup symbols which are inserted into a web page. The code informs the web browser how the words and the images on a web page should be displayed to the user. Each single markup code is known as an element or a tag. A web browser can read the HTML file and then render it into a visible web page. It also describes the structure of a website in a semantic manner. As a result, HTML is not a true programming language but a markup language.

Other languages, like XML, are also used to write web pages but HTML is the most common. This is how it works in essence:

- HTML is the language that two computers use to communicate with one another over the Internet

- The web sites that we see are the result of those communications

HTML is a "spoken" language between a client and a server computer:

- The client is the computer that is in use by the person who is surfing the Internet, like the computer that you use every day

- The server stores website and distributes them across the web

You will often see these termed as "client-side" and "server-side" which means that something has taken place either on the client computer or on the server. For example, if someone said to you, "the script is running on the client-side" it would mean that the script is running on the client computer.

Let's assume that a customer wants to purchase a specialized dog collar and you happen to sell them. The customer will fire up his computer (the client), open the Internet, open a search engine page and type in "Specialized dog collars." He clicks on search and, should a perfect world exist, your website will be the first one on the list.

The customer, clutching his credit card, clicks on the link to go to your home page. The client, not the customer, sends a request over to the server, asking it to send your home page to the client. The server will look for and find a file with a name of "index.html" or maybe "index.htm." This is the default name of your home page and this is what will be sent to the client. That index file will then request everything else it needs, such as pictures, so that your home page is shown off to its absolute best.

The History of HTML

The histories of the Internet and HTML are completely intertwined with each other having been developed together. Tim Berners-Lee developed what was to be called HTML for use in the first website and the first web server in the world. It was written sometime in 1990, and became available to the public 1991. Over the years, HTML has undergone several iterations. It was in 2000 that HTML was officially standardized as the markup language to be used for developing web pages for the Internet.

HTML5 is what HTML was supposed to have been. The very first web browser was called Mosaic and it was brought out in 1993. The following year, Netscape came out. This was based on Mosaic and it was the beginning of a new world for the Internet. Both

Mosaic and Netscape used HTML but, until HTML 2.0 was released, there was no "gold" standard for the language.

HTML 2.0 came out in 1995 and HTML 3.0 followed in 1997. Two years later came HTML 4.0 and that is where it stayed, with HTML 4.0 the standard to work by, until now. In January of 2008, we saw the very first working draft of HTML 5.0 and it quickly gained very broad support from most browsers. HTML 5.0 is still a work in progress and it is expected to take several years before it can be implemented fully.

In more ways than one, HTML 5.0 isn't all that different to version 4.0. Some tags, like the <font> tag, do not work in 5.0 and there are a few other things that have been changed and tidied up but, rather than introducing any major new changes, that is all HTML 5.0 has done so far – tidies up all the loose ends.

What HTML5 isn't:

It's nothing like print. With print, we see images and text embedded onto paper as a series of colored dots. On the Internet, images are handled in a different way. They are sent over the net as discrete files and are displayed on your screens as illuminated color pixels. The text is displayed as it is, as text.

Why can we not display each pixel with a defined color and then have the web page uploaded as one single image? There are two reasons why we can't do this:

1. The web page would be far too big and would take forever to download.

2. Spiders, like Googlebot, would have no chance of reading them.

HTML5 is also nothing like Math. It isn't a new kind of geometry. Computer science aspires to have the logic and the order that goes with Math but, so far, it has been unable to match it.

In the last 20 years or so, some very smart people have been making HTML from scratch and they continue to do so. While version 5.0 is most definitely better than the earlier versions, it still has its flaws and these will raise their heads at the times when you least expect or want them to so be prepared. In short, if you do not expect to see Euclid Geometry-style perfection, you will not be disappointed.

In spite of the changes to the language, there are still a few features in HTML5 that were present in the first version of HTML. This is the latest version of HTML, and it was launched in October 2014. When you wish to learn HTML, it will actually be HTML5 that you will be learning.

Basics of HTML

All HTML documents should start with a document type declaration i.e. <DOCTYPE html>

HTML document begins with <html> and ends with <html> only

The visible part of the HTML document is between <body> and </body>

Let us look at the below example of a simple HTML document for a better understanding of the language:

<!DOCTYPE html>--------------defines the document

<html>-------------------------signifies root element of HTML page

<head>-------------------------includes meta information about the document

<title>Page Title</title>--- specifies title of the document

</head>

<body>--------------------------consists of visible page content

<h1>My First Heading</h1>-defines large heading

<p> My First paragraph.</p>-defines a paragraph

<body>

<html>

Elements to create a HTML Web Page

In order to create a simple web page, you need to know the basic elements and tags such as those that are used in defining the layout among other things. These elements are used in nearly all web pages to give a structure to the content placed on them. Here is what you need to know to start creating simple web pages.

1. **Page Title-**All HTML pages must have their own page title. It acts as the name for the document. The page title helps the user understand what they can expect from that page. Moreover, it will be used as the default title when the page has been saved to the bookmarks of the browser. The page title is not shown in the actual body of content of the web page.

The syntax for the page title element is given below.

<Title>...</title>

The title element is always placed inside the head element. Example:

<!DOCTYPE html>

<html>

<body>

<h2>The title attribute</h2>

<p title= "These are the tooltips">

```
</p>

</body>

</html>
```

2. **Paragraphs**-The Page Title does not affect the actual content placed on the web page. However, the Paragraph element most certainly does. You can type in a message on separate lines in HTML. However, they will always get printed on the same line by the browser unless you make use of the Paragraph element. After all, HTML is not about presentation but rather about meaning. The syntax for this element is given below.

<p>...</p>

On inserting a piece of text inside these tags, you can ensure that the text will be considered as a separate block of text. It will get displayed as a new paragraph. An example of its use is given below.

```
<! DOCTYPE html>

<Html>

<Head>

<Title>List of Animals</title>

</head>

<Body>
```

```
<p>this is a list of animals. </p>

<p> it is quite interesting. </p>

</body>

</html>
```

3. **Line Breaks-**The line-break tag is used for separating a single line into two. Unlike other elements, line-breaks do not have any closing tags as there is no content involved when a line is being broken. You may find it easy use line breaks quite often. However, you must avoid so especially when two pieces of text are meant to be completely separate from each other. In such situations, the paragraph element will suit you better. The tag for line breaks is <br> and an example of its use is given below.

A List of Animals

And Other Animals

4. **Lists-**HTML allows you to organize your content into lists to make the content more presentable on a web page. There are actually three kinds of lists available in HTML. They are ordered list, unordered lists and, finally, definition lists. Out of them, a definition list is a bit advanced. Therefore, we will only consider the ordered and the unordered lists here. Both of these lists work in a similar manner. However, unordered lists

are used when the list items are non-sequential. They are generally preceded by bullets. However, ordered lists are used when the items have to be listed sequentially. As such, they are preceded by incremental numbers.

The unordered list element can be defined by the following syntax.

<ul>

<Li>...</li>

<Li>...</li>

<Li>...</li>

</ul>

The syntax for ordered lists is similar. The only difference is in the tag used as you can see below.

<Ol>

       <Li>...</li>

       <Li>...</li>

       <Li>...</li>

</ol>

The <li>...</li> tags are used to define each item that will be placed on that list.

In order to understand the ordered and unordered lists in HTML, you can take a look at the following example.

<! DOCTYPE html>

<Html>

<Head>

<Title>my first web page</title>

</head>

<Body>

<h1>A Short List of Animals</h1>

<Ul>

<Li>Cat. </li>

<Li>Dog. </li>

<Li>Horse. </li>

</ul>

</body>

</html>

When you get your browser to display this page, you will find that the names of the animals have been displayed in the form of a bulleted list. You can change the <ul>...</ul> tags into <ol>...</ol> tags. This will cause the display of the list to be changed into a numbered list from a bullet list.

In HTML, you have the ability to create a hierarchy of lists. This means you will be creating a list within another list. This allows you to organize the content better. You can take a look at the following example to understand how you can create a hierarchy of lists.

<! DOCTYPE html>

<Html>

<Head>

<Title>my first web page</title>

</head>

<Body>

<h1>A Short List of Animals</h1>

<Ol>

<Li>

Cat.

```
            <Ul>

            <Li>Siamese cat</li>

            <Li>Persian cat</li>

            <Li>Burmese Cat<.li>

            </ul>

</li>

<Li>

Dog.

<Ol>

<Li>Golden Retriever</li>

<Li>Tibetan Mastiff</li>

<Li>Pug</li>

</ol>

</li>

<Li>Horse. </li>

</ul>

</body>
```

</html>

As you can see in the example, when you are creating a hierarchy of lists, it is possible to use unordered and ordered lists together. You can use as many levels of lists as you want.

5. **Links**-Links are central to our use of any website or web page. As such, it helps to know how you can implement them in HTML. After all, links are what enables the Internet to bring everything together. As you already know, the first two letters in 'HTML' mean hypertext. This can be defined as a system of linked text.

When creating a link in HTML, you need to understand a few things. An anchor tag will be used for defining a link. You will need to add the link's destination to the anchor tag to create a functional link in HTML. The destination of the link can be defined with the help of the 'href' attribute in the tag.

It is possible to make the link absolute which means that it will take you to a specific website. For example, you can link to 'HTTP: //www.amazon.com' or "HTTP: //www.google.com'. The syntax, in this case, would be as follows.

<a href="http://www.amazon.com ">Amazon</a>

Alternatively, it can be used to point to another file located in the same directory. For example, let's suppose that you have created another HTML file called bird.html and saved it in the same directory. In that case, you can use the following syntax for creating a link to the file.

<a href="bird.html">The List of Birds</a>

Keep in mind that you can link to all kinds of files and not just HTML files. More importantly, it is possible to link to a file over the internet as well.

You can also point the link to another section of the same page. You may have already seen this in action if you have used Wikipedia. In order to create such a link, you need to add an id attribute to a tag. It is possible to add such an attribute to nearly all tags. Look at the following example to understand how it works.

<p id="bird">The List of Birds</p>

...

<a href="#bird">Check the List of Birds</a>

Once the link has been clicked on, the page will scroll to the element, in this case, a paragraph, which contains the corresponding id tag.

Steps to create HTML page

As we have gone through the basics of HTML language, let's look at a step by step process of creating an HTML page.

1. Text editor- Open a text editor of your choice, example- notepad and create an empty text file.

2. HTML code- Copy and paste the HTML code into your new text file

3. Save – Click the file and save it with HTML file extension, e.g. "nameyoulike.html"

4. Demo- Do a double click on the file to view it on any web browser.

Hello World Example

To help you get a better understanding of the structure and syntax used in HTML5, you should take a look at the following example. After all, there is no better way to learn than by practice. The following is a hello world example, a type of program that is often used in programming to provide an introduction to the fundamentals of a language.

```
<! DOCTYPE html>

<html Lang="en">

<Head>

<Meta charset="utf-8">

<Title>HTML5: Hello World Example</title>
```

```
</head>

<Body>

<h1>Hello World</h1>

</body>

</html>
```

As you can see, this is actually quite a simple program. On executing this code, a web page will open up, displaying the text, "Hello World." Due to the simplicity of code in HTML5, you can actually understand what is going on in the program.

First, the language of the text to be displayed on the web page is defined to be English. Then, the character encoding of the HTML document is defined with the charset attribute. Finally, the text to be displayed is mentioned inside the body tags.

The Structure of HTML Documents

A HTML document is a file that contains hypertext markup language. An HTML code is based on tags that provide instructions to format a document. I will be talking more about the different tags shortly but first, this is the basic layout of an HTML document.

In any HTML document, the document type element, also known as doctype, is mentioned. Its aim is to ensure that the browser renders the HTML in the standards mode so that it works in the correct manner. The use of doctype also allows validation software to know which version of HTML the code should be validated against.

After the doctype, the opening HTML tag is used. This opens the HTML code and is closed with the closing HTML tag. They serve as a wrapper for the entire document. As a result, the closing HTML tag will always be the last thing in any HTML document.

Following the HTML element, the head element is inserted. This wrapper contains all the information or the metadata of the document. This is followed by the title element, which is used to define the title of the page as it will be shown in the menu bar.

After the closing of the head element, the body element is used. This contains the actual content that will be present on the page. As you can see, there is only a header element in the body element of the Hello World example.

Now let's break and look at each of the tags in more details so that you understand them better:

The html tag

This is the tag that tells the computer that it contains HTML content. With one or two very important exceptions, more about those later, every tag must be opened and it must be closed. Look at this example:

\<html\> - opening tag

\</html\> - closing tag

There is just one difference – the addition of the (/) in the closing tag.

A tag is nothing more than a container and the HTML tag is telling the computer that everything in between \<html\> and \</html\> is a code that conforms that HTML standards as dictated in the doctype declaration. So, everything in between the opening and the closing tag has the attributes that the tag gives it. We can modify those attributes, as you will see later.

Within the HTML tag, there are two other tags that are equally as important:

\<head\>

\<body\>

The Head Tag

This tag contains information that the browser and the spiders will need. Each website has a human audience and an audience made up of 'crawlers', 'bots' or 'spiders'. While human viewers will not see anything of any importance in the head tag, the crawlers and bots will. Every search engine has a crawler – the Google one is called Googlebot – and these are constantly roaming, surfing the Internet, going from a link on one site to another, collecting information and indexing it all as they go. Every search engine has its own algorithm that takes this information and works out which pages relate to specific search terms.

If a website reads well to the crawler, it has a better chance of appearing higher up in the search results and this is known in the trade, as SEO or Search Engine Optimization. Books, reams of books have been written on this subject and, although I really can't go into it in depth here, it will be touched on throughout.

What I will say is this – the most important thing you should do, if you do nothing else as far as SEO goes, is to make sure your title tag is good. You won't see the title tag on the page but it will show across the top of the browser in the address bar and it also shows in a button on the taskbar, wherever that is situated on your computer – most are along the bottom of the screen. The title tag should be heavy on keyword BUT it must also be readable – less than 64 characters if possible.

The next most important thing is to be realistic. At this stage, you will find it virtually impossible to get a decent ranking on the most popular search terms or words. For example, if someone were to search for 'bakeries', it's highly unlikely that 'Jake's Bakes" will show up. However, if someone were to type in "jakes bakes" that website would appear at the top of the search results. That website will make money because the time was taken to use the right keywords and the right title tag. These are crucial steps but it is quite shocking how few web designers take note of them.

Also included in the head tag are meta tags. There are two very important ones to take note of:

- charset meta tag

<meta charset= "utf-8>

- description meta tag

<meta name= "description" content- "the head tag has the title and the meta tags – these are important for the search engines and contain the information needed for the web browser to display the page properly.">

The charset is telling the browser the letter type that the page is written in. If you have used another language rather than English for your website, you must make sure you choose the right charset. The one describes above, <meta charset= 'utf-8"> is for plain old English.

The description meta tag will, on occasion, show up in a search and is helpful for SEO purposes.

The Body Tag

In the body tag is a copy of all the code that generates exactly what you see in your browser window when you open a web page.

Most of the work here is done on code that is found in between the opening body tag and the closing body tag. This is where the fun starts, along with no small amount of aggravation!

Generally, you will find that web designers fall into two categories – those who are interested in design and those who are interested in computer science. These two are worlds apart yet, to be a good web designer you must have some expertise in both areas. That isn't something you will learn straight away but it will come in time – provided you stick to one simple rule – Keep It Simple!

This is applicable for design and code writing. In fact, if you can learn how to write simple and clean code, you will find it results naturally in a simple clean design, and that works the other way as well. If your code is messy and somewhat convoluted, not only is it difficult to read, it is also hard to tweak and to debug and, no matter what you do you will end up spending time doing both of these – the trick is to keep that time to a minimum.

There is so much you can do on a website, loads of smart things that get you saying, "now, that would be cool!". It's all very well having wonderful thoughts; putting them into action is another thing entirely, especially when you are a beginner.

Remember that I told you a tag is a container. Occasionally they will have text in them, occasionally an image but, more often, a tag will contain more tags and it is these tags that have the images, the text and more tags in them. Even trying to keep it simple, it can still get quite complicated very quickly.

The Heading Tag

The heading tag is what tells the spiders, like Googlebot and people who visit our website how important each element of your page's content is. When the internet first came about, it was used mostly in universities. To start with, anything that was published looked like an outline and not like the kind of article you would read in printed publication.

Page titles were put inside an <h1> tag, displaying text in a larger size. Subtitles were put into an <h2> tag or any other tag up to an <h6> - each one with ever decreasing text size and ever decreasing importance.

<h1>h1 tag</h1>

<h2>h2 tag</h2>

<h3>h3 tag</h3>

<h4>h4 tag</h4>

<h5>h5 tag</h5>

<h6>h6 tag</h6>

Header tags have grown in popularity alongside the internet. For a start Google loves header tags and let's face it, if Google wants them. Google will get them! In terms of web designing, Google is the king, we all know it. When you design your website, you are doing it with one primary goal – to get people to visit your site and to keep them once they get there. Google does the first bit – it gets them to your site.

Google, and all other web search engines, all rank the relevancy of sites in several ways. Head tags are just one of the things that they consider then your website is indexed and they all assume that the content in an <h1> tag is more important than the content in an <h2> tag and so on down the rankings.

So, wouldn't it make sense to stuff your page with <h1> tags? Wouldn't that give it a higher ranking? No, it wouldn't! Google hates people that do that and they will penalize or ban them altogether so be smart when you are making your web page. Spit your headings down into the order of importance and put the most important in the <h1> tag. Not only will you get higher rankings, your site will be much better designed.

Keep in mind that the heading tag is important but so is the title tag. Things can get very complicated when you are designing a website in HTML, so use your heading tags wisely to keep things in order.

The Paragraph Tag

On a website, this sentence would be in a <p> tag.

As would this one be...

And this one too ...

The paragraph tag is most likely one of the most useful and one of the most commonly used of all the tags. While it has been in existence ever since HTML was first introduced, many web designers won't have used it. The reason for this is that in the previous version of HTML we used the <font> tag instead but, although it still works in HTML4, it has been replaced by the paragraph tag in HTML5. Any web designer who has not kept up to date with the way that HTML standards are developing will find that this is one of the biggest changes between the two versions.

Now it's time to make a web page.   At the end of the book I have included two hands-on projects for building a web page but, for now, just copy this into any text editor:

```
<!DOCTYPE html>

<html lang="en">

  <head>

   <meta charset="utf-8">

   <title>My very first web page</title>

  </head>
```

```
<body>

  <p>My very first web page</p>

  </body>

</html>
```

This code has been indented so it is easier to read and far easier when it comes to debugging. Unlike other computer programming languages, indentation does not affect how the elements of the code function. It is good practice to indent just so you can read your code better – trust me, you will be grateful for it later!

A word on text editors – use TextWrangler on Mac or Notepad on Windows – Microsoft Word is NOT a text editor despite some people thinking it is.

Save this file to the desktop and call it my-very-first-web-page.html. Now open it from your desktop by double clicking on it and, in an ideal world it will open in your primary browser.

Did it not work?

Did you use MS Word as an editor, even though I told you not to? Only use a proper text editor, not a word processor.

Did you save it with a .html extension? By default, a text editor will save any file with a .txt file extension unless you tell it otherwise. Change it in your text editor and it should work.

Did you save it on your desktop? It doesn't really matter to be fair; you can save it anywhere so long as you can find it again.

If it still doesn't work, don't get all frustrated. Stop, take a short break or leave it until tomorrow. Things often look much easier in the cold light of a new day.

Now, if it did work then congratulations are in order – you have just created your very first web page. Now do a bit of editing on it – change what is in the <p> tags, add a new one and put some heading tags in. Don't forget that, whenever you make a change you must save the file again and then refresh the browser for those changes to take effect.

There is one important rule you must learn in HTML5 and it is a grammar rule:

You can nest tags but it is important that you open and close them in order. Look at these examples:

Example 1:

<body>

  <div>Cool:</div>

  <p>Correct</p>

</body>

Example 2:

```
<body>
  <div>Cool:
    <p>Correct</p>
  </div>
</body>
```

Example 3:

```
<body>
  <div>Not Cool:
  <p>Incorrect</div> </p>
</body>
```

Example 4:

```
<body>
  <div>Not Cool:
  <p>Incorrect</p>
</body> </div>
```

The <div> tag may be closed before the <p> tag is opened, as in example 1, or after you close the <p> tag, as I example 2.

However, it cannot be closed if the <p> tag is already open, as in example 3, nor can it be closed once the <body> tag is closed.

Take some time out to understand the business of nesting. Remember that tags contain other tags and similar to a Russian Doll, they must open and close in the order they are in. You may struggle to keep track of what you need to put there but practice will see you right on that one.

Types of HTML

The newest version as we have mentioned above is HTML 5. This version can be divided into three categories. The types define how HTML is used.

1. Transitional- It is the most common type of HTML and has a flexible syntax, spelling and grammar component. This type of HTML has been used without syntax restrictions. The browsers support a best effort approach for tags, so if tags are not spelled correctly the browser will not correct the error but will display the content.

2. Strict- This type requires the closing of all opened tags. Strict HTML is essential on phones since they have limited processing power. Also, the pages load faster if the codes are clean and free of error.

3. Frameset- It allows developers to create a medley of HTML documents i.e. multiple documents are connected to a single screen. This type is usually used to create menu system of the website.

Elements in HTML

In HTML, a basic element will have two markers located around a block of text. It is also possible for an element to have other elements inside it. In fact, this is the case for all HTML documents. After all, the main sections of the code are always put inside the HTML elements. However, there are a few exceptions, as certain elements cannot contain any text or other elements. The img element is one such example.

Elements in HTML5

In HTML5, a few changes were made to the elements. They are now separated into a range of element content categories. In HTML5, the elements are marked with the help of start and end tags. The closing tag always contains a slash whereas the opening one does not. In HTML5, the element names are insensitive to cases. As such, you can write them in uppercase or even mixed case without any problems. However, it is a good practice to use lower case for element names. Listed below are some of the semantic and structural elements of HTML 5:-

1. <article>-defines an article

2. \<aside>- defines content to the side of the content page.

3. \<bdi>- a part of the text that may have been formatted in a different way than the rest of the text.

4. \<details>- gives additional details that the user may use or hide

5. \<dialog>- describes dialog box or window

6. \<figcaption>--gives a caption for \<figure> element

7. \<figure>- defines content like illustrations, photos, diagrams, code listing etc.

8. \<footer>- defines a footer for a section or the document

9. \<header>- describes the header for the document

10. \<main>- main content of a document is defined

11. \<mark>- shows highlighted or marked text.

12. \<menuitem>- an item from the menu which user can use from the popup menu bar.

13. \<meter>- measurement within a known range

14. \<nav>- shows navigation links in the document

15. \<progress>-shows the progress of a task

16. \<rp>- describes what to show in the browser

17. <section>- defines a section or a part of document

18. <summary>- visible heading for a <detail> element

19. <time>- gives date and time

20. <wbr> - possible line break.

Attributes in HTML5

In HTML, elements can have attributes that set the different properties of the element and change its behavior. Some attributes have to be defined globally, and they can be used with any element. However, there are others that are meant to be used with certain specific elements only. Attributes are meant to be specified in the start tags. They can never be used in the closing tags.

Like elements, attributes in HTML5 are insensitive to cases. They can be written in any case you want. However, you should practice using only lower case for them.

Most of the attributes along with their possible values are defined in the HTML specifications. As such, you do not have the ability to create your own attributes. If you do so, it will make the HTML invalid. After all, it can confuse the user agents and even cause issues in the correct interpretation of the web page.

Standard Attributes

Listed below are some of the standard attributes used in HTML5

Attribute	Options	Functions
align	Left, right, center	Aligns the tag horizontally
bgcolor	Hexidecimals, numeric, RGB values	A background color is placed behind an element
accesskey	User defined	Defines a keyboard shortcut to access an element
class	User defined	Differentiates an element for the use with cascading style sheets
height	Numeric value	Defines the height of images, tables or table cells.
Item	List of elements	It is used to group elements
spellcheck	True or false	Specifies if element requires spelling pr grammar check
width	Numeric value	Defines width of images, tables or table cells
title	User defined	"pop-up" title for elements

Some Interesting features of HTML5

HTML5 has various features that a modern day website requires. Although there has been no change in the programming model of HTML, however, HTML5 is easy to implement. It is a language which can be called as backward compatible, in the sense that these new features can be ignored in case they are not supported by a browser. However, most of the commonly used browsers support HTML5, listing below few of them:

a) Google Chrome 10.0 and higher

b) Firefox 4.0 and above

c) Internet Explorer 8.0 and above

1. Multimedia Support in HTML5- The first and foremost feature of this programming language is that it supports multimedia files i.e. both audio and video files which can be played on the browser. Given below is the sample syntaxes:

Syntax to play video:

<body>

        <video src= "video path" controls>

        </video>

</body>

Syntax to play audio:

```
<body>

<audio src= "audio location" controls>

        </audio>

</body>
```

2. New Input Element Types – In data driven web applications, these input elements play an important role. These help in receiving the input in a required format. Some new inputs have been added in HTML5, and few of the existing ones are file, password etc. Below is an example of one of the useful input introduced:

```
<input id = "EmailIdInput" type= "email"/>
```

3. Canvas- It is a rectangular area that allows pixel level operations such as drawing a box, line, circle, performing graphics etc. Below is the sample syntax:

```
<canvas id= "mybox" width= "100" height= "100">
```

4. **Custom Data Attributes** - There is a new feature available in HTML5 which is the introduction of custom data attributes. They can be added in a hidden manner from the user and can be used later by Java Script functions. These attributes need to start with 'data-', and they can be named as per your needs.

Example-

<div class= "example" data-subject= "maths" data-level= "complex">

...

</div>

5. **Editable Contents-** The end users can edit HTML control's content under this feature. It also allows developers to create web pages with sections like HTML editor, notes etc. In order to use this feature, add the following to the control panel of HTML:

contentEditable="true"

6. **Range validators and required -** "required" attribute is used on the input controls and it ensures that until the value is entered for input control form will not get posted. Sample syntax:

<input type= "text" name = "TextBox" required/>

Under the range validators, validation is reached only when minimum and maximum values are specified for the input control. The value entered should be within the range otherwise the form will not get posted. Below is the sample syntax for this feature:

```
<input type= "number" name = "Number of Items" min= "5"
max= "10" required/>
```

7. **Placeholder and autofocus attributes**- The automatic focus is on page load under this attribute. Placeholder feature displays the value like a watermark unless the focus is shifted to the input control. Below is a sample syntax:

```
<button id= "SubmitButton" autofocus></button>
```

```
<input type= "text" name = "text box"
        Placeholder= "Please enter text..."/>
```

8. **Preload videos**- This attribute enables the browser to preload the video. So, if the user visits the page that has been specifically made to play the video and it is preloaded already, then it saves a lot of time to the visitor.

9. **Geo-Location**- This feature of HTML5 lets you share your location with websites of your choice. It works well on smart phones.

10. **Figure element**- By using this feature one can semantically associate an image with their captions. We simply need to add <figcaption> element. Below is a sample of this element:

```
<figure>
```

```
<img src= "path/to/image" alt= "About Image"/>
```

```
<figcaption>

<p> This is a beautiful scenery. <p>

<figcaption>

</figure>
```

Advantages of using HTML5

1. **Built in audio/video compatibility**- Nowadays, websites have to be highly interactive so as to keep the audience engaged. Therefore, developers need to include videos, animations, play music and social network sites like Twitter and Facebook into the websites. With the help of HTML5, all this can be done quite easily. It allows the developers to add rich content to the site without using any third party programs.

2. **Improved code and cleaner markup**- Most of the div tags can be replaced with semantic elements of HTML5. Hence, this language offers a cleaner code.

3. **Stylish forms**- The developers can use fancier forms with HTML5. There are different types of text inputs and different fields for different inputs.

4. **Enhanced Semantics-** The semantics have improved in HTML5, which has made identification easy for parts of the page like footers, headers, navigators etc. since they have

specific tags. HTML5 offers standardized codes thus increasing the semantic value of the web page.

5. **Consistency-** As more and more websites adopt HTML5 elements consistency in terms of HTML coding will improve from one web page to another.

6. **Accessibility-** The structure of a web page can be understood in detail with HTML5 by just taking a look at the elements it has.

7. **Web applications made easy-** Once you know the available features of the browser you will be working on, you can use them in your application. The main purpose of HTML5 is to make easy applications with easy drop and drag tools, font-ends and other useful elements.

8. **Offline Cache-** While building a website using HTML5, the developer can specify the files which should be cached by the browser. So even if you are offline, the page that you have visited in the past and want to visit it again, will still load.

9. **Client side database-** Cookies impact the response time of web pages. With HTML5 it is better managed by using local storage and session storage instead of cookies. However, it is not a permanent database but enables temporary storage of structured data.

10. **Mobile optimization-** HTML5 is optimized for the creation of mobile applications and websites with complete functionality. Mobile Internet users can browse easily without scrolling horizontally.

Disadvantages of HTML5

1. HTML5 is only supported by modern browsers.

2. Most parts of the language are stable; however, it is still considered to be work in progress. This means that any element can change anytime.

3. Like Apple and Google, HTML5 does not have an adaptation control. There is no central location from where users can look and purchase HTML5 apps.

4. HTML5 faces media licensing issues.

5. HTML5 cannot create dynamic output and the security features are limited.

This chapter must have given you an insight into the basics of HTML and its functionalities. Now let us look at some frequently asked questions on this programming language for more clarity on the topic.

FAQ's

1. What is the purpose of HTML5?

Answer: HTML5 was designed to overcome the shortcomings of XHTML, HTML4 and HTML DOM level2. The language focuses on delivering high-quality content without additional plugins. The new structural element tags of the language give a better semantic support to the overall web page structure. The error handling has been simplified and it also provides backward compatibility. HTML5 can be implemented across platforms such as tablets, Smart phones, and PC.

2. Can HTML5 specifications be implemented on all types of browsers?

Answer: As of now, no browser supports all the aspects of this language. Therefore, it becomes imperative for the developer to ensure that the aspect being used will be supported by the browser on which the content is to be displayed.

3. Are HTML tags and elements different?

Answer: Elements in HTML communicate to the browser how to deliver text. Whereas, when elements are surrounded by <> (angular brackets) they become tags.

4. What do you mean by DOCTYPE and what is the new form for it?

Answer: This term tells the browser what kind of HTML is used on a web page. Browsers use DOCTYPE to determine as to how to make a web page. The new form is <!doctype html>

5. Describe the correct usage of the header, section, article and footer in HTML5?

Answer: Header- It is used to contain navigational and introductory information about a section of a given page. This information can be either on author's name, date, time, section heading, table of contents or any other navigational information.

Section- It is a flexible container that holds the content and shares common information.

Article- It holds self-contained composition which can be recreated independently outside the page without losing its meaning. Example: blog posts, news stories etc.

Footer- This contains information which is to be displayed at the end of the content and may also contain additional information about that section. Example: copyright information, related links etc.

6. What kind of media elements are supported by HTML5?

Answer: It supports both audio and video tags.

7. Are there any new image elements included in HTML5?

Answer: Yes, there are two new image elements they are; WebGL and Canvas. Canvas contains graphics whereas Web Graphics Language (WebGL) is a free cross platform that is used for generating 3D graphics in browsers.

8. Why do we need data- attributes?

Answer: This attribute is a new addition to the language which assigns custom data to an element. This element is good to store private or sensitive data that is exclusive to an application or a page and there are no matching elements and attributes for it.

9. What are some standard API's that comes with HTML5?

Answer: Some of them are: Text Track, Media, Application Cache, Command, User Interaction, Data Transfer, Constraint Validation and the History API.

10. What is the difference between HTML browser cache and HTML5 application cache?

Answer: Caching in HTML5 application creates an offline version and stores files such as images, HTML files, CSS and JavaScript locally and thus increases the speed of the website as compared to the traditional HTML cache.

Overall, HTML 5 is an exciting programming language for creating powerful browser based applications. It lets you format the text, create links, add graphics, input tables, forms, frames etc. and save it in a text file that any browser and read and display.

Now that you have gained insight into HTML5 you can easily use and implement this programming language for creating websites.

CHAPTER 3
SOME MORE FEATURES OF HTML

Now that we have taken some time to look at HTML and some of the different features that come with it, it is time to work on learning some more about the different parts that come with it. We are going to take some time to look at the attributes of HTML, the formatting rules, phrase tags, comments and more.

Attributes

In the previous chapter, we took some time to talk about simple tags, but there are also some tags that work with attributes. These are used in order to add in some extra information. By adding in this attribute, you are able to define what characteristics of an element in HTML. These attributes are going to be added inside of the opening tag of your element and each one is going to consist of two parts, the value and the name.

The name inside of the attribute is the property that you are looking to add. For example, if you are working on the font element you may want to add in the color and the size to tell the system what kind of font you want to use. The paragraph tag is going to use the align attribute that will let you decide how to align the paragraph.

On the other hand, the value is something that the property takes and then sets it into the content. For example, you can give the size attribute that you are using and then give it a number. The values and names that you are using with the attributes are considered case sensitive and you do need to be careful when you are using them. A good example of how to align the attributes in a paragraph tag include:

```
<!DOCTYPE html>

<html>

<head>

<title>Align Attribute Example</title>

</head>

<body>

<p align="left">This paragraph is aligned left.</p>

<p align="center">This paragraph is aligned center.</p>

<p align="right">This paragraph is aligned right.<p>

</body>

</html>
```

The above code is going to display with the following output:

This paragraph is aligned left

This paragraph is aligned center.

This paragraph is aligned right.

There are many different types of attributes that you can choose to go with including general attributes that work with different parts of the code, the core attributes, and so much more. They basically help you to leave a bit of information inside the code to tell the compiler what it should add into the page.

Phrase Tags

When you are working inside of HTML, there are phrase tags that are designed to carry out a specific job. These are going to be similar to some of the other basic tags that you have used, but they can help you to get so much more done inside of the code. Let's take a look at how a few of these can work for you:

Emphasized text

There are times when you want to emphasize a group of words that you are using. You want to make sure that the reader is able to see them and understand that they are important. In order to make sure that the HTML compiler knows that you would like to emphasize a word or a group of words, you would need to use the

... element to show this. A good example of how this would work includes:

```html
<!DOCTYPE html>

<html>

<head>

<title>Emphasized Text Example</title>

</head>

<body>

<p>The following word uses an <em>emphasized</em> typeface.</p>

</body>

</html>
```

With this code, you will notice that the word emphasized is the one that will have the emphases on it during your writing.

- *Strong text*

If you would like to make sure that a word or words inside of your code are strong and that they stand out from some of the others inside of the document, you will want to make sure to uses the code for strong text. This one is pretty simple; you will just need to use the ... element and place the word or words that you would like to have strong in the middle of them. You can make the string as long as you would like in between them, just make sure that you are using the right element to do it.

- *Abbreviation*

There are times when you would like to make sure that you are abbreviating some of the words in your text. This happens a lot if you are using a name or another word that people would recognize as being the same even in the abbreviated form. You can teach the compiler to find all of the full written out parts of the word and then have it limit it down to the abbreviation if you would like. In order to abbreviate, you would just need to use the <abbr>...<abbr>.

- *Acronym*

You can even do this in the form of an acronym. There are many times in your coding when you would like to write out something as an acronym, such as writing out HTML rather than the whole meaning of the word. You would be able to just use the <acronym>...</acronym> to make this happen.

You will be able to keep doing this with all the special things that you want to add into your code, you just need to be careful to get them to work the proper way. You should find out the keyword for what you would like to do and then place the string of text that you are working on inside and use the syntax from above. There is so much that you are able to do with this option and with the right keyword, you can make it all happen.

Meta Tags

Another thing that you will need to work with is the meta tags. These are the additional important information about the document and you will be able to determine what this metadata is all about. The META elements can be used inside the code to add in some value and name pairs that are used to describe the HTML document properties and can include some options like a number of times, date of creation, expiration date, a list of keywords and more.

All of these are going to use the tag of <meta> to get the work done. This bag is an empty element, which means that you won't need to go through and add in the closing tag like we did with the other examples. The tag is going to carry all the right information inside of the attributes. The good news is that you are able to add in multiple meta tags to the document and they will not change how the HTML document looks. Whether you add them in or not will not matter when someone is looking at the page.

You are able to use the <meta> tag in the header in order to add in this additional information inside the web page. There are a few attributes that are allowed to be placed inside the meta tag, in addition to the core meta attributes, including:

- Name: this is the name of the property. You can name it anything that you would like such as author, description, generator, revised, and keywords.

- Content: this is going to tell the compiler what the value of the property is.

- Scheme: this is going to specify what scheme is used to interpret the value of the property.

- http-equiv: this is used for an http response message header. It can be used to set up a cookie or to refresh the page.

You are able to also use this meta tag in order to specify which keywords are important inside of the code. These can then be used by various search engines when they are indexing the web page. Basically, this is going to help you out to be ranked higher in a search engine search. Let's take a look at an example of how this would work. In this example, we are going to add in the metadata, meta tags, and the HTML as the important keywords in the document:

<!DOCTYPE html>

<html>

<head>

<title>Meta Tags Example</title>

```
<meta     name="keywords"     cntent="HTML,   Meta   Tags,
Metadata"/>

</head>

<body>

<p>Hello HTML4!</p>

</body>

</html>
```

The output that you are going to get from the code that we just wrote is "Hello HTML5!".

- There are quite a few things that you will be able to do with the meta tags that can make organizing your code so much easier than before. Some of the most common options to using the meta tag include:

- Document description: this is when you would like to add in a small description about the document. Take special care when writing this because it is often used by a search engine when it determines rankings.

- Document revision date: this one is going to hold on to information about the last time that you updated or edited the document. The web browser is going to use this information any time that you try to refresh the page.

- Document refresh: you can teach the browser how to refresh your web page after a specific period of time has gone by just by using the meta tag. Then the browser will continue to refresh the web page all on its own to keep the information current.

- Page redirections: sometimes you will need to tell the browser to go to another web page. In these situations, you can again use the meta tag to tell it where to go. You can also tell the browser that it needs to redirect if it is put on hold for too long, and you can figure out how long it should wait.

- Setting up cookies: cookies are basically pieces of data that are going to be stored in small files on the computer. They are going to be exchanged between the web browser and the web server. These will be useful because they help to keep track of any information that your web application may need at some point. You are able to store the cookies on the client side of things with the help of the meta tag. This information will then be used later on by the web servers when they want to keep track of the customer visits to the site.

- Setting up the author name; if you would like to make sure that your name or someone else's name is on the web browser, you can use the meta tag to help this happen to.

The meta tags really can help you to do so much more when it comes to the code you are working on. They have a lot of power and it is meant as a way to help you to not only organize the pages that you are working on but to also make sure that the web search engines are able to find you when your client is looking for information that you have. These are really categories that you should concentrate on because they will make a big difference on whether the client is going to be able to find you or if they will pick another website to visit.

Comments

Comments are an important thing to add into your code. They are basically parts of the code that your web browser is going to ignore, but this doesn't mean that you should never use them. It is a good idea to write in comments any time that you would like to explain something that is in your code. The more complicated the code is, the more likely you are to need lots of comments to be added in. Comments also help to make the code easier to read, helps others who are looking at the code have a chance to understand what is going on, and can tell others what you are doing inside. The web browser is going to just ignore the comments that you write as long as you use the right symbols, so you can write out as many of these as you would like.

If you would like to write out a comment inside of your code, you would just need to use the tag <!--...→. You can put any string of text in here as you would like to help explain that part of the text or to make sure that other programmers know what is going on.

Let's take the time to look at the way that you would be able to write out comments in your HTML code:

```
<!DOCTYPE html>

<html>

<head> <!—Document Header Starts→

<title>This is the document title</title>

</head> <!—Document Header Ends→

<body>

<p>Document contents codes here.</p>

</body>

</html>
```

With the code that we just wrote here, the code is going to ignore the comments, which are the ones that say where the Document Header Starts and Ends, but it will show up everything else. Right now, when you type in the code and ask the web browser to execute it, you are going to get the output of "Document content goes here."

One thing to note about comments is that you are not allowed to place one comment inside of another comment. This is going to confuse the web browser and can result in a mess over time and an error. You should also make sure that there aren't any spaces in the beginning of the comment string or this can result in an error as well.

There are times when you would want to write multiline comments. The ones that we talked about above were short and only took up one line, but how do you work with it when the comment is longer and needs to take up more space than just the one line. This is pretty simple in the HTML language. You just need to make sure that you use the same tag as before. You can start out with the <!—part and then just keep writing out the code until it is done, no matter how many lines it ends up taking up. Once you are done, make sure that the ending of this tag (the → part), is at the end of the string of text so the web browser knows when you are done.

Let's take a look at how you would be able to write out the multiline comment inside of your code:

<!DOCTYPE html><html>

<head>

<title>Multiline Comments</title>

</head>

<body>

```
<!—This is a multiline comment. You are able to make it last for
as many lines as it needs, whether it is two or more lines.-->

<p>Document content goes here...</p>

</body>

</html>
```

And it is as simple as that. We are using the same symbol to get this done, we just need to make sure that we are putting them in the right order and following the same rules as we did with the first option.

What are the conditional statements?

It is possible to work on conditional statements in some forms of HTML code, mainly on Internet Explorer. The other browsers are going to have trouble with these and will often ignore them. You will find that conditional instructions are the best when you are working in Internet Explorer because they are going to give some more conditional instructions to the browser. A good example of how you would write out a conditional comment includes:

```
<DOCTPE html>

<html>

<head>

<title>Conditional Comments</title>
```

```
<!—[if IE 6]>

Special instructions for IE 6 here

<![endif]→

</head>

<body>

<p>Document content goes here...</p>

</body>

</html>
```

There are times when you will want to use different browsers in your HTML code. If you do need to use a different version of the Internet Explorer, you may need to use a different kind of style sheet. Conditional statements can make this easier to accomplish.

Working on Images

There are plenty of instances when you will want to add in an image to your document of HTML. If you want your web page to have a picture on it, you would need to use the right code to make this happen. Pictures can enhance the ideas that you are talking about, break up the text a bit, and really helps to make it easier to get ranked in search engines. In this section, we are going to spend some time talking about how to work with images in your HTML document to make the document really shine.

- *Inserting images*

You will be able to insert as many images into your web pages as you would like, you simply need to be able to use the <img> tag to make this happen. This is an empty tag, which means that you only need to give the list of attributes that you would like to add in, which in this case means the URL or link of the image, and then close it up without a closing tag. Now, we will try out an example of how to make this work inside of your HTML document. The HTML file that we will work with is the tested.htm and the image file that we are trying to get is the test.png. Both of these files are going to be put into the same directory.

```
<!DOCTYPE html>

<html>

<head>

<title>Using Image in Web page</title>

</head>

<body>

<p>Simple Image Insert</p>

<img src-"/html/images/test.png" alt="Test Image"/>

</body>

</html>
```

This is going to help you to bring up the image that you want into the web page that you are using. You can insert as many different pictures as you would like into your web page, just make sure that you know the location of the image file that you want to use and that you use a syntax like this one to get it done. You will find that the HTML syntax is going to be able to support several different types of images including GIF, PNG< and JPEG. The correct file name of the image will need to be placed inside of the src attribute and remember that the name of the image is case sensitive to you may want to just copy and paste it to avoid issues or rename it to something simple.

- *Setting the location of the image*

So, at this point, we have taken a look at how to add a picture into your code, but what happens when you want to put it in a specific spot of the code. To start, it is a good idea to make up a separate directory for these images. We are going to make sure that we save the HTML file inside of the text.htm in the home directory. Inside of the home directory, you will be able to create your own special directory for the images and you will be able to store all of them in there. Here is an example of how you place the image in the right location, which in this case is going to be the /html/image/test.png.

<!DOCTYPE html>

<html>

```
<head>

<title>Using Image in Web page</title>

</head>

<body>

<p>Simple Image Insert</p>

<img src="/html/images/test.png" alt="Test Image" />

</body>

</html>
```

- *Setting the size of your pictures*

Sometimes, the image that you are working with is going to be too big for the area that you are working on and other times you may want to make it a bit bigger so that your user is able to see what is inside of it. You are able to be in charge of the height and width attributes of your image and in HTML, we are going to do them based on a percentage of the actual size of the picture, or you can do it in terms of pixels. A good example of how you would be able to do this includes:

```
<!DOCTYPE html>

<html>

<head>
```

```
<title>Set Image Width and Height</title>

</head>

<body>

<p>Setting image width and height</p>

<img src="/html/images/test.png" alt="Test Image" width="150" height="100"/>

</body>

</html>
```

With the example above, we are producing an image that is about 100 pixels tall and 150 pixels wide. You can always make changes to this later on if you find that it isn't working the way that you would like or it stretches out the wrong way compared to the original picture.

These are just a few of the different things that you are able to do with the pictures when you are trying to add them into your HTML document. You can not only change the size and insert them, but you can add in some extra pictures, such as more than one, into the same document, you can add borders around the picture, and so much more. Decide how you are going to want the picture to look at the end, and you will be able to pick the right code to make this happen.

Creating a Table in HTML

There are many times when you would like to add in a new table inside of your HTML document. You may want to list out certain information in the table or use it for another purpose. Creating a new table doesn't have to be that difficult. A table inside of HTML will be able to contain many different types of data like other tables, links, text and even images. You will just need to use the <table> tag. If you would like to create new rows inside of your code, you would need to use the <tr> tag and then, if you would like to create some new data cells, you would use the <td> tags. Here is a good example of how you would create a brand new table inside of your HTML document.

```
<!DOCTYPE html>

<html>

<head>

<title>HTML Tables</title>

</head>

<body>

<table border ="1">

<tr>

<td>R1, C1</td>
```

```
<td?R1, C2</td>

</tr>

<tr>

<td>R2, C1</td>

<td>R2, C2</td>

</tr?

</table>

</body>

</html>
```

This is going to create a table that has all the information that we listed in the code within it. You will be able to change up the information that you put into the table and add more columns and rows that you would like to add into the table. You will find that this is a quick method that you can use in order to create the table that you want to use inside of your HTML document.

There are a lot of different things that you are able to add into the tables. You can use codes in order to add a header to the table, to work on making the cells of the table bigger than before, to add in a background to the table to make it easier to read on the HTML document, and so much more. You are able to make the table work any way that you would like with just changing up the code a little bit.

Lists

You will have many times when you are able to use lists inside of your HTML document. There are three main ways that the HTML code will allow you to make some of these lists including the following:

- <ul>: this is a list that is unordered. All of the items are going to be listed on the page using plain bullets.

- <ol>: this is a list that is going to be ordered. This means that it is going to use different numbers and schemes for making sure that the items are listed in the right way.

- <dl>: this is a list of definitions. This list is going to be arranged in a way that is similar to how they would be done inside the dictionary.

Let's take some time to look at the different kinds of lists that you are able to work on with your HTML code so that you are able to get the most out of them and figure out when you are able to begin using each of them in your own code.

- *An unordered list*

When you are working with an unordered list, you are working with one that can be defined as a collection of related items that don't have a special order or sequence. An unordered list can be created by using the <ul> Tag. Every item that you present inside of the list will have a bullet to help mark it. A good example of how this would work includes the following;

```
<!DOCTYPE html>

<html>

<head>
<title>HTML Unordered List</title>

</head>

<body>

<ul>

<li>BMW</li>

<li>Nissan<li>

<li>Jaguar</li>

<li>Mercedes</li>

</ul>

</body>

</html>
```

When you take the time to type this into the compiler and execute it, you will be able to see the following output on the screen:

- BMW

- Nissan

- Jaguar

- Mercedes

You will be able to add in as many parts to the code as you would like to make a small list or one that is really long. It is all up to you, but you would use the same format and add in as many parts of the list as you would like to have inside the list.

- *Ordered lists*

There are times when you will want to make a list that is printed out with numbers rather than doing the bullets like in the last example. You would just need to create what is known as an ordered list in order to get this done. You are able to use the <ol> tag any time that you would like to create an ordered list. When you create one of these lists, you will find that the numbers are going to start out with one and then each element is going to go up by one. You will also be able to tag the elements with <li> like the last one. A good example of what you will be able to do when you write out this code includes:

<!DOCTYPE html>

```html
<html>

<head>

<title>HTML Ordered list</title?

</head>

<body>

<ol>

<li>BMW</li>

<li>Nissan</li>

<li>Jaguar</li>

<li>Mercedes</li>

</ol>

</body>

</html>
```

When you type this code into your compiler and ask it to execute it, you will get the following output:

1. BMW

2. Nissan

3. Jaguar

4. Mercedes

- *The definition list*

And finally, the other kind of list that you are able to use is the definition list. Both the HTML and XHTML documents are going to be able to support the list type that is a definition list. All of your entries that are placed inside of the definition list are going to look similar to what you would find as listings in a dictionary or an encyclopedia. Definition lists are a great way to present out terms, parts of a glossary, and other value or name lists that you want inside the HTML document. Some of the tags that you will be able to use for your definition lists include:

<dl>: this is going to be the start of your definition list.

<dt>: this is one of the terms that you will use.

<dd>: this is the term definition.

</dl>: this is the end of the list that you would like to use.

(Tutorials Point)

So now that we know a bit more about the definition list and how it is going to look on the screen, let's take some time to look at the type of code that you are able to use to get the right results:

<!DOCTYPE html>

<html>

```
<head>

<title>HTML Definition List</title>

</head>

<body>

<dl>

<dt><b>HTML</b></dt>

<dd>This stands for Hyper Text Markup Language</dd>

<dt><b>HTTP</b></dt>

<dd>This stands for Hyper Text Transfer Protocol</dd>

</dl>

</body>

</html>
```

Take some time to put all of this into the compiler and then try to execute it. If you put in the right information, you will be able to see the following information come up on the screen:

HTML

This stands for Hyper Text Markup Language

HTTP

This stands for Hyper Text Transfer Protocol

Working with the colors of your page

You have some options when it comes to the colors that you would like to add into your page. You will be able to just leave the color as plain white if this is the easiest for the code that you are working on, or you can change up the colors to really pop out the color. If you choose the right colors, you are able to make the web page look better and it is more likely to attract some more users to the page. Colors can be added to the different parts of the page based on using the <body> tag. This tag has a few different attributes that you are able to use in order to determine the color that you would like to use. Some of the attributes that you are able to choose from with this tag include:

- Bgcolor: this is going to set the color that goes in the background of the page.

- Text: this is going to help you to change the color of the text in the document.

- Alink: this is going to change the color that comes up for the selected or active links.

- Link: this is going to help you to set the color for any linked text that you are using.

- Vlink: this is going to set a new color for any of the visited links. This means that the color will change once you click on a link on the page.

Let's look at some of the other methods that come with using color inside of your HTML document so you will be able to use them properly.

- *Methods for color coding*

Inside of HTML, you are able to make changes to the color of the web page. There are three main methods that are available for helping you to do this and these methods include:

- Color names: you will be able to pick out the names of the colors specifically. The colors you can name out include blue, green, and red.

- Hex codes; these are six digit codes that are going to represent the different colors that you would like to use.

- Color decimal or percentage values: this is the value that you will be given when using the rgb() property.

Let's take a look at what these all mean and how you will be able to find the perfect color for your needs using each of the methods.

- *Color names*

When you would like to add in some color to your background, you are able to specify it by using its real name. There are 16 basic colors that are used on the World Wide Web Consortium and they are going to be usable in most of the modern browsers that you would like to use. Some of the bigger browsers can accept more colors, sometimes up to 200 different colors. The most common colors that you will be able to use and which are supported by most of the major browsers include:

Black

Yellow

Red

Maroon

Gray

Lime

Green

Olive

Silver

Aqua

Blue

Navy

White

Fuchsia

Purple

Teal

Now it is time to look at an example of how you would use the HTML tag in order to change the color of the background simply by using the right name to go with it. \

```
<!DOCTYPE html>

<html>

<head>

<title>HTML Colors by Name</title>

</head>

<body text="blue" bgcolor="green">

<p>Use different color names for body and table and see the result.</p>

<table bgcolor="black">

<tr>

<td>

<font color="white">This text will appear white on a black background.</font>
```

```
</td>

</tr>

</table>

</body>

</html>
```

(Tutorials Point)

Take some time to type this into your compiler and see what comes up on the page. You should notice that there are different colors that show up based on what you write into the code, with the table being in one color, the font in another, and the background in another. You can change this up as much as you would like to get the answers you want or the right colors to look nice on your code.

- *Hex codes:*

It is also possible to represent a color in your code in hexadecimal within the code. This is going to be when you represent the color with 6 digits, and each color is going to have its own unique 6 digit number. For example, the code RRGGBB, is 6 digits and it is going to have the first two values be red, the second two will be green, and the last two will be blue. All of the values of these colors will be started with the # sign. Some of the common representations that you may use in your code include:

Black = #000000

Red = #FF0000

Green = #00FF00

Blue = #0000FF

Yellow = #FFFF00

Aqua = #00FFFF

Purple = #FF0FF

Grey = #C0C0C0

White = #FFFFFF

The RBG Rules

Another option that you are able to use is the rgb() property. Here the R is going to be red, the G, is going to be green, and then the B is blue. They are going to be given values based on how much of each other needs to be in place in order to make the color that you would like. For example, Black means the absence of color so you would have 0 for all of the colors. This is a good one to do if you would really like a specific color, but it is also one that a lot of browsers don't support so it is often not recommended. If you would like to use the RGB rules, here are some of the values that can be useful:

Black= = rgb(0,0,0)

Red = rgb(255, 0, 0)

Green = rgb(0, 255, 0)

Blue = rgb(0, 0, 255)

Yellow = rgb(255, 255, 0)

Aqua = rgb(0, 255, 255)

Purple = rgb(255, 0, 255)

Grey = rgb(192, 192, 192)

White = rgb(255, 255, 255)

All three of these methods are a good way to make sure that you are adding in colors correctly to the code and that they end up being the exact color that you want. The first two rules are often the ones used because they are supported across many different browsers, but you are able to choose the one that is the best for you. Mess around with these a bit on your browser and learn how to make them work for you.

Links

Another thing that you may want to do inside of your HTML document is to add in some hyperlinks. These are special links that are going to redirect the user to another page on your website, a different spot on the same page, or even to another web page to help prove the point that you are trying to say inside of the document. Using hyperlinks are a great way to show more information to your user and can even help you to get ranked higher than before. You are able to use them by either using text or images that are present inside the web page. Let's take some time to look at how you would do hyperlinks inside of your HTML document.

- *Linking documents*

If you would like to specify a link inside of your document, you will need to use the <a> tag. If you put the right link in between the tags, you user will be able to click on the link if they would like to and then they will be redirected to the right spot. Here is a good example of what you would do if you wanted to add in a link to the HTML document:

<!DOCTYPE html>

<html>

<head>

<title>Hyperlink Example</title>

</head>

<body>

<p<Click following link</p>

```
<a href=http://www.google.com target=”_self”<Google</a>

</body>

</html>
```

When you type this code into your HTML document, you are going to get an output link on the page and when you click on this link, you are going to be sent over to the Google homepage. You are able to do this with any link that you would like to add into the document. You would just use this same idea inside of the code and you can add in as many links as you would like.

There are so many things that you are able to do when you are working on an HTML document. This is a great way to create some of your own web pages and make sure that they are going to work the way that you want. Sure, you are able to use a premade website if you would like, but often these are going to be harder to use and will make it difficult to get exactly the way that you want. But when you know how to code your own web page, it is easier than ever to create the perfect web page, no matter what topic you are putting into it.

CHAPTER 4
HTML BEST PRACTICE GUIDE

The following are some of the best practices that you, as a beginner, should learn:

1. Make sure your tags are always closed. It used to be common seeing things like this:

<li>A bit of text here.

<li>Some more text here.

<li>You see what is happening.

Do you see how the wrapping UL/OL tag has been left off? Many people also chose to leave the closing LI tags off as well and that is simply bad practice. Always ensure your tags are closed otherwise you will be plagued with glitches and validation issues.

This is better:

<ul>

  <li>A bit of text here. </li>

  <li>Some more text here. </li>

<li>You see what is happening. </li>

</ul>

2. Always make sure the correct DocType is declared.

The DOCTYPE is situated at the top of the page, in front of the opening HTML tag. It is used to inform the browser whether the page is XHTML, HTML or both so that the markup can be interpreted correctly

3. Avoid the use of inline styles

When you are working away on your markup, you might find it easier and just a little bit tempting to take an easier route and sneak some styling in there.

I'm going to put this text in red so that it stands out and everyone notices it!

It might look harmless but this is actually pointing out that there is an error in your practices. When you create the markup, forget about styling; wait until the page has been fully coded first. Finish the markup and then put in a reference from the external style sheet to the P tag.

This is better:

#someElement > p {

  color: red;

}

4. Make sure your external CSS files are inside the head tag

You can technically put your stylesheets wherever you want but the standard HTML specification recommendation is the put them inside the head tag for the document. The main benefit to this is that your pages will appear to load much faster.

<head>

<title>My Favorite Kinds of Beans</title>

<link rel="stylesheet" type="text/css" media="screen" href="path/to/file.css" />

<link rel="stylesheet" type="text/css" media="screen" href="path/to/anotherFile.css" />

</head>

5. JavaScript files are best at the bottom

Remember one of your goals is to make sure your pages load faster for a user and if it has to load scripts, a browser has to wait until the whole file is loaded. This results in a user having to wait longer for any progress.

If your JS files have only got the purpose of adding functionality, put them at the bottom, just in front of the closing body tag, like this:

```
<p>And now you know my favorite kinds of beans. </p>

<script type="text/javascript" src="path/to/file.js"></script>

<script type="text/javascript"
src="path/to/anotherFile.js"></script>

</body>

</html>
```

6. Inline JavaScript is so 1990's! Forget about it

One more very common practice from many years ago was to put JavaScript commands inside tags, especially with image galleries. All that happened was an 'onclick' attribute would be added as an appendment to the tag with the result that the value would become equal to a JS procedure.

Instead, this code should be transferred to an external JavaScript file then you should use 'addEventListener/attachEvent' to listen for that event or, if you use a jQuery framework use the click method.

```
$('a#moreBeansInfoLink').click(function() {

  alert('Do you want to learn more about beans?');
```

```
});
```

7. Never stop validating

There are quite a few people who don't understand what validation is all about. Validation is meant to work in your favor because it helps you to see what is going on and where you are going wrong. When you first start out download the Web Developer Toolbar from W3C and use it constantly. Validate all the time and don't stop until there is nothing left to go wrong.

8. Download Firebug

Firebug is a fantastic plugin for website creation, providing you with some powerful JavaScript debugging and the chance to see which elements are getting padded out unnecessarily.

9. Use Firebug!

It's one thing downloading it but you really need to use 100% of the capabilities that Firebug offers. Most people use no more than about 20% and if you are one of those you are not doing yourself any favors. If you don't know how to use it, check out the internet for some useful tutorials.

10. Your tag names should always be in lowercase

You can capitalize them if you want:

<DIV>

```
<P>Here's a fascinating fact about beans. </P>

</DIV>
```

But, really, you shouldn't. It doesn't serve any real purpose and it can hurt your eyes after a while. Stick to lower case – this is better.

```
<div>

<p>Here's a fascinating fact about beans. </p>

</div>
```

11. Make sure you use those H1 - H6 Tags

Many coders tend to slack out on this but you should really make use of all of them. For SEO purposes, if nothing else, use an H6 in place of a P tag when it is right to do so.

```
<h1>This is a really vital fact about beans! </h1>

<h6>Small, but not insignificant fact about beans goes here. </h6>
```

12. If you are doing a blog site, keep H1 for the title of the article

Do figure out what works best for your own site; a small percentage of people use H1 for the logo but, in all honesty, you should save them for the article titles – definitely best practice in terms of SEO.

13. Download ySlow

ySlow is a Yahoo extension for Firebug and, once downloaded and activated, it analyzes the specified website. It will return a kind of report card telling you where your site needs to be improved. It might be a little harsh at times but it is in your best interests

14. Use an unordered list to wrap navigation with

Every website has some kind of navigation section on it and, while you can format it like this:

```
<div id="nav">

 <a href="#">Home </a>

 <a href="#">About </a>

 <a href="#">Contact </a>

</div>
```

In terms of semantics though, this is not recommended. Your task is to come up with the absolute best code that you possibly can so why would you even think of styling a list of the navigation links in any way other than with an unordered list? The UL tags are designed to contain item lists so this is much better:

```
<ul id="nav">

  <li><a href="#">Home</a></li>

  <li><a href="#">About</a></li>

  <li><a href="#">Contact</a></li>

</ul>
```

15. Learn how best to target Internet Explorer

There is no doubt that, at some point you will find yourself losing your rag with Internet Explorer but you need to understand how to target it if you are going to become best pals. When your primary CSS file is finished, the next step is to come up with a unique 'ie.css' file. Then it can be referenced just for Internet Explorer in the following way:

```
<!--[if lt IE 7]>

  <link    rel="stylesheet"    type="text/css"    media="screen"
href="path/to/ie.css" />

<![endif]-->
```

What this is saying is, if the user has Internet Explorer 6 or lower, this stylesheet should be imported. Otherwise nothing needs to be one.

16. Make sure you use a really good code editor

It doesn't matter whether you are using a Mac or Windows PC, there are loads of good code editors that will do the job you need them to do. If you want to start simple, go with Notepad on Windows, which should already be built in and TextWrangler on Mac.

17. When your website is finished, compress it.

Zip your Javascript and CSS files so that you can cut the size by at least 25%. Don't do this while you are still developing your website, wait until the work is done first. There are plenty of online compression tools so make use of them to cut your bandwidth.

18. Cut, cut and cut some more

When you first start learning, you will naturally want to put as much in as you can. One common beginner mistake is to wrap every single paragraph in a <div> and then wrap another <div> around it for safety. This is not efficient, so when your markup is complete, go over it at least twice more and look for ways to cut some of the elements on the page.

19. Every image needs an 'alt' attribute

One of the easiest things to do when you are coding is to ignore the need for those alt attributes inside the image tags. However, these attributes are incredibly important, both for validity and for accessibility. So, make sure you take the time to fill them in. This is a bad example:

<IMG SRC="cornImage.jpg" />

This one is much better:

<img src="cornImage.jpg" alt="A corn field I visited." />

20.   Keep late hours

Most programmers find that they lose track of time when they are coding and suddenly, it's all gone dark outside and inside. For many, these are the times when everything seems to come together when a problem you have been wrestling with for what seems like hours will suddenly go right.

21. Look at source code

There is no better way to learn than to copy something someone else has done. All programmers are copiers to start with; to a certain extent, you have to be to understand what everything does. It's only later that you will start developing your own methods and styles. So, go to good websites and take a good look at the source code. Ask yourself, how did they do that? What code did they use? Don't steal what they have done but copy bits and learn. Many of the best effects on a website come from plugins – when you look at the source code, examine the HEAD tag to find out what the script name is. Then search for it on the internet and use it in your own code.

22.   Make sure you style every element

This is particularly true for those who are designing a website for a client. You may not have used a blockquote but your client might. Just because you don't like ordered lists, your client might. Create one page that shows off the styling of every single element.

23.   Make use of Twitter

Twitter is all we seem to hear about these days and, to be honest, it can be somewhat annoying. The original idea for Twitter was to let people post what they were up to but this seems to have slipped by the wayside and it has turned into a serious marketing tool. Get yourself a Twitter account and look for web developers who are working in the area you are studying. Follow them and check out the links they post because they will often contain some very useful information.

24.   Learn how to use Photoshop

There are those who don't think that Photoshop has any place in web development but it is, in fact, one of the most useful tools you can ever use. In time, it will become the most important tool that you have at your disposal. Once you have gotten the basics of HTML, CSS, etc. down, then get onto Photoshop and learn how to use it properly – it's a great tool for mockups!

25.   Learn all the HTML tags

There are dozens of these tags that you are not likely to come across on a regular basis but that doesn't mean you don't need to learn them. Make sure you are fully familiar with and know how to use every single HTML tag. For example, do you know what <abbr> or <cite> are used for?

<abbr> is referencing an abbreviation. For example, you could wrap Blvd inside an <abbr> tag, referencing it as an abbreviation of Boulevard. <cite> is used for referencing other people's work or the title of a book or article. For example, if you were to reference this book in your blog, you would put the title of it inside a <cite> tag. The only thing you should not use it for is as to reference an author of a quote you may have used.

26.   Get involved in the community

Everyone who is into web development has something to offer to the community – and plenty to learn. If you finally learned how to do something that was bothering you, tell everyone about it. Get involved with web development forums and talk to others – as well as asking questions of the more experienced web developers, you can answer questions for those less experienced than you.

27.   Create a CSS reset file

Some developers say these should never be used but you should get into the habit of creating a CSS reset file. Start by downloading and using one from the web, preferably a popular one and then, as you go along and you begin to learn, start to modify it so it becomes your own. If you can't or don't do this, you are never going to fully understand why your list items seem to be getting padded when you didn't want them to. Stop yourself getting wound up by using a reset file! Something like this:

```
html, body, div, span,

h1, h2, h3, h4, h5, h6, p, blockquote, pre,

a, abbr, acronym, address, big, cite, code,

img, ins, kbd, q, s, samp,

small, strike, strong,

dl, dt, dd, ol, ul, li,

fieldset, form, label, legend,

table, caption, tbody, tfoot, thead, tr, th, td {

    margin: 0;

    padding: 0;

    border: 0;

    outline: 0;

    font-size: 100%;
```

```css
    vertical-align: baseline;

    background: transparent;
}
body {

    line-height: 1;

}
ol, ul {

    list-style: none;

}
blockquote, q {

    quotes: none;

}
blockquote:before, blockquote:after,

q:before, q:after {

    content: '';

    content: none;

}
```

```
table {

    border-collapse: collapse;

    border-spacing: 0;

}
```

28. Get your elements in a row

Try to get your elements lined up as best as you possibly can. Look at a design that you particularly like. Do you see how the headings, the icons, paragraphs and the logos all line up with something else? This is what you should be striving to achieve.

29. Don't start using a framework just yet

Whether they are for CSS or JavaScript, a framework can be a truly great thing but you should avoid using them when you first start to learn. Although you can learn JavaScript and jQuery together, you can't do this with CSS. Using one when you first start will only leave you confused and disheartened so leave the frameworks for when you are experienced enough.

CHAPTER 5
UNDERSTANDING CSS: STYLIZING THE INTERNET

The function of HTML is to create web pages. However, it is incapable of ensuring a proper presentation of the content. In order to make the web page stylish and improve its presentation aspect, you need to use a style sheet language such as CSS.

What is CSS?

What CSS stands for Cascading Style Sheets is a design language which simplifies the process of ensuring that your web pages are presentable. It takes care of the looks of the web page. With it, you can control various aspects of the page such as the font style, the text color, column sizes, paragraph spacing, layout, background images or colors and other designs. You can also enable variations in the display to cater to different screen sizes and devices.

CSS is generally used for designating the visual style of web pages and, also, user interfaces that have been written in HTML or XHTML. However, you can also use the language for all kinds of XML document types.

CSS was created to allow the document content to be separated from document presentation including colors, fonts, and layout. By separating them, some things can be improved upon such as content accessibility. It also enables enhanced control and flexibility in various aspects of the presentation. It also allows multiple HTML files to share the same formatting.

The separation also makes it possible to deliver the same page in a range of styles to suit different rendering methods such as in print, on-screen and by voice. It also becomes possible for the users to create a different CSS file to override the one specified by the creator of the web page.

Currently, the latest version of CSS in use is CSS3. CSS3 brings quite a few new features to the language while building upon the previous version. We will be concentrating only on CSS3 in this book.

History of CSS

Hakon Wium Lie first proposed CSS on 10th October 1994. There were many other style sheet languages which proposed around the same time. Finally, CSS1 was released in the year 1996 and Microsoft Internet Explorer became the first browser to support CSS. This language was specifically developed to hold the content on the web while HTML was there to create the documents on the World Wide Web.

The concept of style sheets was not new. However, the existing languages required style sheets to come from different sources on the web whereas on the other hand CSS influenced the document style by way of cascading styles. The term cascading means the ability to combine multiple CSS files to decide a style for one page.

Let us look at some advantages and disadvantages of CSS

The Advantages Offered by CSS

There are some considerable advantages in using CSS. Some of them have been mentioned as follows.

- **Timesaver**: One of the biggest advantages of CSS is that it saves a considerable amount of time in web development. A CSS can be written only once for an HTML page. It can then be reused over and over again for multiple HTML pages. A style can be defined for each element in HTML and then applied to a variety of web pages.

- **Easy Maintenance**: CSS allows you to maintain multiple pages very easily. You can easily make a global change by changing the style in CSS. The corresponding element in all the HTML pages will get updated automatically.

- **Faster Loading Pages**: It is not necessary to define tag attributes in HTML multiple times when CSS is being used. One CSS rule needs to be written for a tag, and it can be applied to all occurrences of that specific tag. This decreases your code considerably which leads to faster downloading times for each page.

- **Better Styles**: Compared to HTML, CSS offers a much bigger range of attributes. This allows you to improve the looks of the HTML page considerably more than what would have been possible if you had used HTML attributes only.

- **Caching**: CSS allows web applications to be stored locally by means of an offline cache. This allows you to view websites offline. The cache also enables faster loading of the pages and improves the overall website performance as well.

- **Multiple Device Compatibility**: You can use style sheets to optimize your content for a range of devices.

- **Global Standards**: The fact is that the attributes available in HTML are being reduced. Instead, CSS is being recommended as the alternative. As a result, CSS is being used for all web pages to ensure compatibility with web browsers of the future.

Disadvantages of CSS

1. **Different levels of CSS**- The language comes in different levels from CSS1 to CSS3 which has resulted in confusion amongst the developers about which version should be used.

2. **Fragmentation**- in the CSS what might work with one browser may not work with the other. Therefore, the web developers have to first test the compatibility by running the program across multiple browsers before a website is made live.

3. **Lack of security**- CSS doesn't have a built in security system since it has an open text-based system. So, anyone who has a read-write access to the website can alter the CSS file, links or change the formatting whether by mistake or by design.

Getting Started with CSS

To get started with CSS one needs a text editor, a modern browser and some experience. Let us look how CSS works:

When a document is displayed in a browser, it must combine the style information with the content in the document. The document gets processed in two stages:

1. Browser converts CSS and the markup language into the Document Object Model or DOM, which represents the document in computer's memory.

2. The content of the document is displayed by the browser.

In the markup language, elements are used to define the document's structure. As we have learned in the previous chapter, elements are marked using tags. Most of the elements in CSS have a starting and an ending tag. The tags begin with the symbol "<" and end with ">".

However, depending on the markup language few elements, where "/" comes after the name of the element and they have only single or start tag. Each attribute, element, and run of text become the node in the tree like structure of DOM. These nodes are defined by their relationship to other DOM nodes i.e. there are some elements that act as a parent for child nodes and child nodes might have some siblings.

Understanding the document object model will help you to debug, design and maintain CSS. Let us look at an example to explain this model-

In a document, the <p> tag and its end tag create a container:

<p>

   <strong>C</strong>ascading

   <strong>S</strong>tyle

   <strong>S</strong>heets

</p>

In DOM, P node is parent and its children are text nodes and strong nodes, where Strong nodes are also parents of text nodes.

The Hello World Program in CSS

As with other languages, the hello world program can serve as a good introduction to CSS. You can see CSS in action in the following example.

```
<style type="text/css">

h1 {

    Color: DeepSkyBlue;

}

</style>

<h1>Hello, world! </h1>
```

As you can see, this CSS rule targets the H1 tag of the HTML page. In this case, we change the color of the H1 text with the help of a color value known as DeepSkyBlue.

Creating and Applying CSS to an HTML File

Before you can start creating your own CSS for your HTML file, you need to know how you can implement CSS in HTML. In order to do so, there are four options available to you. They are listed below.

1. Inline

In this method, the style rules are placed directly into the HTML file. The style attribute is used in the tags whose styles need to be changed. Here is an example showing the inline method.

...

The result of this rule will be that the text of that paragraph becomes blue.

Using this method can have a disadvantage too since it bloats HTML and website maintenance becomes a little difficult. However, it works well in some situations. For example, in case you are using a system where you do not have any access to CSS files then you can simply add your style rules to the elements.

2. Internal

If you want to implement a particular style rule for the whole page, you should opt for the internal method. It is also known as the embedded method. The rules are placed inside the head element. You can see in the following example how it works.

<! DOCTYPE html>

<Html>

<Head>

<Title>CSS Example</title>

<Style>

```
    P {

        Color: green;

    }

    A {

        Color: blue;

    }
</style>

</head>

</html>
```

When you use this, you will find that all the paragraphs are written in green while all the links appear blue.

The drawback to this approach is that every time styles have to be downloaded as someone visits the web page. This gives a slow browsing experience to the user. However, this method has its own advantages as well. The whole page exists as just one file since CSS is part of HTML document. It is useful in cases where you are sending a web page to someone via email or it will be used as a template for blogging. Another advantage to embedded method is that the dynamic styles can be generated at the same time when a database is used to generate the page content. The colors are inserted into headings and other elements into the CSS rules which are embedded on the page. It allows users to change the colors without editing CSS in their blog from the admin page.

3. External

As the name suggests, this method involves the creation of a completely separate CSS file. This allows the external styles to be applied to the entire website or multiple pages. This is, in fact, the best way to implement style rules in HTML> After all, HTML is meant to be a completely separate document that is free from presentation aspects. This is why inline and internal methods are avoided. A basic example of a CSS file is given below.

P {

    Color: green;

}

A {

    Color: blue;

}

This file needs to be saved in the same directory as the HTML page that it is supposed to stylize. You can choose any name for the CSS file, but common naming conventions dictate that it should be named as style.css to make it easier for you. Once the file has been saved, you can link your HTML file to it. The following code shows how you can link the HTML file and the corresponding CSS file.

```
<! DOCTYPE html>

<Html>

<Head>

<Title> Example</title>

<link reel="stylesheet" href="style.css">

...............
```

On saving the HTML file, it will become linked to the CSS file named style.css that is saved in the same directory. Any changes you make to the CSS file will get reflected when you open the corresponding HTML file.

Advantages of linking to separate CSS file is that if you want to make a style change across the website then only once you need to make the change in your single CSS file. Another advantage of using this method is the speed. On the first visit to the website, the user's browser downloads the HTML of the current page along with linked CSS file. When the users navigate to other pages of the website their browser only needs to download the HTML page, thus increasing the browsing speed.

4. **Importing a CSS file from within CSS-** This import rule allows attaching a new CSS file from within CSS itself. To do this one has to simply do the following-

@import "newstyles.css';

Here, you can write your CSS file name instead of "newstyles" and ensure that you include correct path. For example, we have a 500-page website and we want to add a second CSS file to all the pages. So instead of editing all 500 HTML files by adding another CSS link we can simply import the second CSS file from the first file and hence saving a lot of time.

The Syntax of CSS Rules

In CSS, we do not write programs per se. After all, it is a style sheet language. Instead, we write rules. A CSS will have a set of style rules which will be interpreted by the browser before applying them to the associated elements in the HTML document. A style rule, as you have already seen, comprises of three parts.

Selector: This is the HTML tag on which the style will be applied.

Property: This is a kind of attribute of the HTML tag. All HTML attributes get converted into their respective CSS properties.

Value: Each property has a corresponding value attached to it.

For example:

h1 {color:brown;font-size:12px;}

In the above example:

h1 is the selector

color is property

brown is value

font-size is property

12px is value

The selector points to the element which you want to style. The declaration block contains more than one declaration which is separated by semi colon and every declaration includes a CSS value and property name which are separated by a colon. A CSS declaration mandatorily ends with a semi colon. The declaration blocks are enclosed in curly brackets.

The basic syntax of all CSS rules is given below.

Selector {property: value}

CSS selectors find the HTML element based on their name, class, id, attribute and more.

Selectors in CSS can be defined in a number of ways. In fact, you can easily choose one that you are comfortable using. Here are a few kinds of selectors and how they are used.

1. The Type Selectors

You will have already noticed the use of this selector in the preceding examples. This allows the rule to be applied to all elements of the same type. In the following example, the green color is applied to all the level 1 headings in the page.

```
h1 {

        Color: #36CFFF;

}
```

2. The Universal Selectors

Instead of selecting elements of a particular type, you can use the universal selector. This will allow you to apply the rule to any element type that can use the given property. The following example illustrates the use of universal selectors. In it, the entire content of the document will be displayed in black.

```
* {

        Color: #000000;

}
```

3. The Descendant Selectors

In some cases, you may wish to apply style rules to a specific element only when that element lies in another specific element. This is certainly possible with the help of descendant selectors. You can take a look at the following example. In it, the style rule will only be applied to the <em> element when it is present inside the <ul> tag.

Ul em {

      Color: #000000;

}

4. The Class Selectors

It is possible to use the class attribute to define the style rules for the elements. With class selectors, elements with that class will be stylized as per the defined rule. Take a look at the example given below.

.black {

  Color: #000000;

}

On using this rule, you will see that all the elements whose class attributes are set to black in the document will have their content displayed in black. At the same time, it is possible to refine the rule future and specify a certain element. Check out the following example.

h1.black {

  Color: #000000;

}

In the above rule, the content will be stylized black but only in the case of <h1> elements whose class attribute has been set to black. It is also possible to apply multiple class selectors to a specific element. Take a look at the following example to see how it works.

<p class="center bold">

Text

</p>

5. The ID Selectors

You can also take the ID attribute into account when defining the style rules for the elements. In this case, all elements that have that specific ID will be stylized as per the rule you have defined.

#black {

    Color: #000000;

}

On using this CSS rule, you will find that all elements that have black as their id attribute will have their content displayed in black. It is also possible to refine this rule further and target a specific kind of element. In the following example, only the h1 tags that have black as their attribute will be affected by the rule.

h1#black {

    Color: #000000;

}

ID selectors are quite useful when they are applied alongside descendant selectors. In the following example, you will see that all the h2 tags will be shown in black only when those level 2 headings are present inside tags that have their id attribute specified as black.

#black h2 {

    Color: #000000;

}

6. The Child Selectors

Child selectors are similar to descendant selectors. However, their functionality is quite different. The example given below illustrates the use of child selectors. In this CSS rule, a paragraph will be displayed in black only if they are the direct child of the

<body> element. If a paragraph exists inside any other element such as <td> or <div>, it will not be affected by this rule.

Body > p {

    Color: #000000;

}

7. The Attribute Selectors

With the help of attribute selectors, you can apply a specific style to an element that has a particular attribute. In the given example, the style rule will be applied to all the input elements that possess a type attribute with a value of 'text'.

Input [type = "text"] {

    Color: #000000;

}

Attribute selectors have one major advantage. In these cases, the element of <input type = "submit" /> will remain unaffected. Instead, the designated color will only be applied to the text fields that are required. Attribute selectors follow certain rules which are listed below.

- P [Lang] –In this case, paragraph elements that have a Lang attribute will be selected.

- P [Lang="en"] –Only those elements whose Lang attribute has the exact value of "en" will be selected.

- P [Lang~="en"] –It will select all paragraph elements which has a Lang attribute containing the word "en".

- P[lang|="en"] –In this case, all paragraph elements that has a lang attribute containing values which are exactly "en", or begins with "en-".

These are the 30 selectors, along with examples, in CSS that you must remember if you want to master it:

8. Multiple Style Rules

In certain situations, you may be required to set more than one style rule for a specific element. CSS allows you to combine different properties and their corresponding values and make a single block of code. You can see how this works in the example given below.

h1 {

    Color: #000000;

    Font-weight: normal;

    Letter-spacing: .3em;

    Margin-bottom: 2em;

    Text-transform: lowercase;

}

As you can see in the example, all the pairs of property and value are separated with the help of a semicolon. If you want, you can keep the rules together in a single line instead of using multiple lines as long as you ensure that they are divided with a semicolon. However, keeping them in different lines enhance the readability of the code.

(CodesCracker)

9. Selector Groups

It is also possible for you to apply a style rule to multiple selectors if you want or require. In this case, the selectors will have to be separated with the help of a comma. You can see this in action in the given example.

H1, h2, h3 {

Color: #000000;

Font-weight: normal;

Letter-spacing: .4em;

Margin-bottom: 1em;

Text-transform: lowercase;

}

The style rule defined here will be applied not only to the h1 element but also the h2 and the h3 elements. The order of the list does not affect the rule.

(CodesCracker)

Using Colors in CSS

When you are stylizing an HTML document, the color will certainly be one of the things you will be implementing. In CSS, you have the ability to choose between 16,777,216 colors for shading your text. Here is how you can implement them in your Style rules.

The Values of the Color Property

In CSS, the value of the color property can be mentioned as a name. Alternatively, you can use a hex code or an RGB code. Some of the ways you can use red as a value for this property is given below. In other words, when the following codes are used with the color property, you will notice that the text is displayed in red.

- red

- Rib (100%, 0%, and 0%)

- rgb(255,0,0)

- #f00

- #ff0000

Certain color names have been predefined in CSS. They include yellow, blue, fuchsia, lime, green, navy, red, white, black, aqua and olive among others. CSS also considers transparent to be a valid value. Other than black and white, you will find that color names are rarely used in CSS style rules. This is due to the high specificity of the names which make their flexibility rather limiting.

The RGB code is made up of three values, each denoting the primary color. The values range from 0 to 255 with the lowest level of the shade being denoted by 0. 255 is the highest possible. It is also feasible to represent these values in the form of a percentage.

The Hexadecimal code makes use of the base-16 number system. Each hex number is prefixed with the hash symbol. In CSS, their length can be of three or six digits. The three digits version is simply a shortened form of the six digits one. You will find that the latter version allows you greater control over the color.

Using the Color Property

When you wish to apply color to the document, you can use one or both of the two properties given below.

- Color: This is used for applying color to the text.

- Background- color: This is used for applying color to the background.

When using these commands, make sure that you have typed color properly. Browsers do not recognize 'color.' Instead, they can understand 'color.' These properties can be applied to nearly all HTML elements.

Stylizing the Text in CSS

The text is another common item that is stylized to improve readability among other things. CSS gives you a number of properties that you can use to alter the looks and layout of the text on the web page. Given below are some of the most commonly used properties in the text.

1. **The font-family Property** - This property defines the font of the text such as Verdana and Times New Roman. When you use this property, you need to make sure that the browser is capable of locating the font that has been specified as the value. This means the font has to be available on the user's computer. If you use a rare or uncommon font, it is possible that your users will not be able to use the file because they don't have the font on their computers. There are quite a few fonts that will always be available on computers such as the Verdana above and Times New Roman along with Arial and Calibri.

On the other hand, you have the ability to mention multiple fonts as the value for this property. You need to separate the values with the help of commas. This allows a browser to search the user's computer for one of the fonts that have been mentioned in a list. Once it finds the correct font, that font will be used for displaying the text.

Keep in mind that the browser will follow the list sequentially. Therefore, in a list that you have specified as Arial, Verdana, serif, the browser will search for trial first and use it if it is found. If not, it will search for the Verdana font and so on. Another point you need to remember is that you need to put the font name in quotation marks if the name consists of two words or more.

Here a simple example showing how this property is meant to be used.

Font-family: Verdana, Arial, "Times New Roman", serif

2. **Font-size-**This property sets the size of the text. You can, of course, set any value that you wish. However, you need to keep the readability of the content in mind. As a result, the text that you want to use as a heading should be of a higher font-size value but also have the appropriate heading tag such as <h1> as well. You should not simply use the HTML paragraph element for them and give them a higher font-size. The most common units that are used to size the text are:

a) px (pixels) - It is an absolute unit and one can increase or decrease the pixel size of the text as per the requirement.

b) ems – font size set for parent element is equal to 1em. It can be used to size anything and not just text. The entire website can be sized using ems and hence will make the maintenance easy.

c) rems- They work like ems, except that the font size set on the root element of the document is equal to 1rem instead of the parent element. It makes easier to work out the font sizes. However, rems is not supported in Internet Explorer 8 or lower versions.

The font-size of an element is in accordance with the parent element. The size of the font for a root element is set at 16px by default across all browsers. Therefore, any paragraph within the root element will have 16px as font-size.

Let us look at this simple sizing example:

When you size your text, it is always better to set the font-size as 10px for the document, so that that it becomes a lot easier to do the math. Now, when you do this the required rem or ems values are then pixel font size, which will be divided by 10 and not 16. Doing that, you can easily size the text according to the requirement. Also, it is always better to list all font rule sets in a selected area of your stylesheet for an easy access.

3. **Font-weight-**This property is used to check if the text is bold. Generally, the values used for this property are either bold or normal. This is to ensure compatibility with older browsers. However, there are other values that you can use such as lighter and bolder. You can also use any value between 100 and 900 with an increment of hundred.

4. **Font-style-**This property is used to stylize a piece of text as italics. The available values for this property are italic or normal.

5. **Text-decoration** -This property is used for defining whether the text should be underlined, have a line running through or over it. If you do not want such effects, you can use the value normal to denote so. The other values available are given below.

- Underline: This underlines the given text.

- Line-Through: This puts a line running through the text.

- Overline: This will put a line running above the text.

6. **Text drop shadows-** There are four properties to text shadow:

a) Horizontal offset of the shadow. It takes most available CSS size and length units. However, px is used in general. This value has to be included.

b) Vertical offset of the shadow. The shadow moves up and down instead of left-right. This value has to be included.

c) Blur radius- shadow is dispersed more widely. In case this value is not included then by default it becomes 0, and that means no blur. This property also takes most length and size units of CSS.

d) The base color of the shadow, which can be taken as any CSS color unit. If this is not included then by default it remains black.

Multiple shadows can also be given to the text by separating multiple shadow values with a comma.

7. **Text-Color-** This property is used to set the color of the text.

8. **Text Alignment-** Text align property is used to align the text horizontally. A text can be aligned right, left, center or justified. Example:

h1{text-align:right;}

When justified text alignment is used each line of the text gets an equal width and the right and left margins are straight. Example:

div{text-align:justify;}

9. **Text transformation-** This specifies lowercase and uppercase letters in a text. By using this property first letter of a word can be written in capital as well. Example:

p.captitalize{text-transform:capitalize;}

10. **Text Indentation-** It specifies the indentation of the first line. Example:

p{text-indent:40px:}

11. **Letter Spacing-** It is used to specify space between the characters in a given text.   The below mentioned example shows how to decrease or increase the space-

h1 {letter-spacing: 5px;}

h2 {letter-spacing: -5px;}

12. **Line Height-** It specifies the space between each line. Example:

p.small {line-height: 0.6;}

p.big {line-height: 1.6;}

13. **Text direction-** It is used to change the direction of an element. Example:

        div {direction: rtl;}

14. Word Spacing- It defines the spaces between words. Example:

H1 {word-spacing: 15px;}

H2 {word-spacing: -10px}

The above-mentioned properties can give you a fair idea of how to stylize your text on a web page. Apart from that, there are many more which can be used once you are comfortable using the basic ones. Listed below are some of them-

Font Style

a) Font variant-switch between normal font alternatives and small caps

b) Font variant ligatures-control which contextual forms and ligatures are used in the text.

c) Font variant numeric- controls the usage of alternate glyphs for fractions, numbers, and ordinal makers.

d) Font stretch- by using this option one can switch between all possible stretched versions of a given font.

Text layout Styles

a) White space- it defines how white space and related line breaks within the element are handled.

b) Word break- specifies whether lines are to be broken within the words.

c) Word wrap- it defines whether browser may or may not break lines within the words to avoid overflow.

d) Writing mode- It specifies whether text lines are laid out vertically or horizontally and the direction of subsequent lines.

Shortcuts in CSS

Now that we have learned the basics of CSS, we are writing certain shortcuts of the language which can be used with practice. These shortcuts can make your code easier to read, load faster and of high quality. Shortcuts are a great way to speed up the process. However, one should be careful while using them since if not used in the proper manner it can give you negative results. Therefore, always analyze whether using such shortcuts would be beneficial or not.

1. Property Grouping- This shortcut enables set of values for a set of properties to be defined in one line instead of different lines.

Example: using fonts

Without grouping	With grouping

h1{
 	
font-weight: normal;
 	
font-size: 20px;
 	
line-height: 12px;
 	
font-family: georgia, tahoma, verdana;
 	
}
	h1 {
	
	font: normal 20px/12px Georgia, Tahoma, verdana;
	
	}

(CodesCracker)

2. Typing on one line- Everyone has a different approach on how to write codes but one thing is common for all, the lesser number of tabs and spaces you use, the faster your code will load. The idea is to create a highly readable code without too much white space. Typing a set of properties on one line can be a solution to this.

Example:

Typing in multiple lines	Typing in single line

p{
 	
color: #4f39ac;
 	
background: #f4f4f4;
 	
line-height: 16px;
 	
}
	P{color: 4f39ac; background: #f4f4f4; line-height: 16px;}

3. Color value shortening- Instead of using the full 6 digit value while declaring the hexadecimal color value for an element, you can shorten it to three. That is possible if color code consists of 3 pairs of repeating digits.

Example:

	Color value shortening shortcut
body {background: #gggggg;}	body {background: #ggg}
h1 {background: #aa5566;}	h1 {background: #a23;}
p {background: #112233;}	p {background: #123;}
#menu {background: #ggaa44;}	#menu {background: #ga4;}

4. Using zeros- You don't need to use pt, px, em or any other measurement types when you use zero

Example:

#menu {margin:20px 0;}

Some tips and tricks for using CSS

1. Try and use shorthand CSS codes that are cleaner and easier to understand.

2. Always write code for standards compliant browser first. After that, you can correct it for IE at the end. Never do it the other

way around since it increases the probability of forward compatibility.

3. The *class* and *ID* selectors often confuse beginners. In CSS language *class* is represented by a "." whereas "#" represents *ID* selector. In short, ID is used on a style that is unique and cannot repeat itself; on the other hand, the class can be reused.

4. It is always better to get an instant preview of the layout while altering the CSS. This way CSS styles can be understood and debugged better.

5. If in a containing block with a fixed height you want to vertically center the text than simply set the line-height of the text to be same as the height of the containing block.

6. For creating fluid images set the max-width on the images to be 100%

7. When there are conflicting instructions are sent to a single HTML element by two or more CSS selectors than a choice must be made as to which styles to apply. This can be done by using CSS specificity calculations which are expressed in the form of (a,b,c,d).

8. Any image that is wrapped with a link will have a border around it. So, to remove the border you can do the following:

9. An image {border: none} or an image {border:0}

10. Always ensure that different link states are set in a particular order. The most common and easy way to remember this has been Love Hate, i.e.-

11. LVHA- Link, Visited, Hover, Active

12. In order to create 3D buttons, then the trick is to give different colors to your element borders. Typically, one or two shades of color changes are needed, but you can experiment with different effects as well.

These are only a few tips and tricks but as you get into practice and with experience there are many more which you can find out on your own. We are writing some frequently asked questions for a better understanding of this dynamic language.

FAQ's on CSS

1. Why are style sheets required?

Answer: Style sheets are required since they provide a great degree of control on layout and display. They reduce the amount of format coding required to control the display characteristics.

2. How do we link the external style sheet?

Answer: It is a template document or a file which can be linked with a number of HTML documents. It is a convenient way of formatting a site. LINK element is used to link file with HTML documents. It is essential that files should have extension as .css

3. How is ID selector different from class selector?

Answer: ID selectors are unique whereas one class selector can be applied to multiple HTML elements.

4. What is the difference between block elements and inline elements?

Answer: The inline elements takes up only the necessary width whereas block elements take up the entire width which is available and have a line break.

5. What fonts are common across all platforms?

Answer: Five basic font families are recognized across all platforms. They are: sans-serif, serif, monospace, cursive and fantasy.

6. Can comments be included in Style sheets?

Answer: Yes, comments can be included anywhere in the style sheets provided there is a white space.

7. Does CSS have any limitations?

Answer: Yes, there are few limitations

a) There are no expressions and column declaration

b) Ascending by selectors is not possible

c) Targeting specific text is not possible

d) There are limitations in vertical control

8. What is the float property?

Answer: Under this property, the image can be moved left or right along with the text which is wrapped around it.

9. Can we remove gap under the images and how?

Answer: Yes, the gap under the images can be removed since images are treated as text as they are inline elements.

img {display:block;}

10.   How can one add comments in CSS?

Answer: Comments can be added by using /* and */ in CSS.

As you may have realized, CSS is quite an easy an easy language to learn. It is designed to define the overall appearance of not only the web pages but the structure of both text and the elements. This chapter would have given you an insight into how to create web pages that offer a rich experience to the users by using cutting edge and standard CSS techniques.

You should have very little problems in picking up the more advanced skills. In fact, you should find it easy to stylize the text in a web page at a basic level.

CHAPTER 6
SOME MORE THINGS TO KNOW ABOUT CSS

While we spent some time above working on some of the basics that come with CSS, there are still quite a few things that you will want to learn how to do with this programming language. As mentioned before, you may be able to do a lot when it comes to the HTML document that you are working on, but simply placing things into the compiler and having them show up on the page is not enough for the web page to get a lot of views on it. You need to have some of the right presentation in place as well to make the page look nice. CSS is able to help you to get all of this done, as long as you learn how to make it work properly.

So now that we know a little bit more about CSS, it is time to start working on some of the other things that you are able to do when working with the CSS language.

CSS box model

All of the elements that you use inside of CSS are going to be seen as boxes. This means that they are going to have a border, margins, padding, and then there will be the actual content that is inside of it all. Then you will be able to change how much padding, margin and border you would like to have around your text when working inside of CSS. You can play around a bit in this language to get the padding right where you would like it and to ensure that the text is not too far away from each other, but still enough distance to make it easy to read.

- *Height and width properties*

These two properties are going to tell you the dimensions of the content area, without including the margin, border, or padding. The values are going to be given in the form of a percentage or a pixel. For example, you may want to make the width and the height of your boxes be 100 pixels. You could also change it to make one or both be 80 percent. If you would like to keep things simple, you will be able to set both the width and height to auto so that the compiler will calculate the values based on how much space you need in order to correctly display the content that is inside the box.

- *Overflow property*

Sometimes your height and width are going to be too small to hold all the information that is inside of the box. By default, the content is going to start going outside the box and it can overlap with some of the other contents. This is going to be bad for the web page because it is going to make it look like a mess and it is not going to be formatted very well. If you would like to avoid this from happening, you will need to use the overflow property. This will help to make the box change size so that all of the information can fit inside and the web page will still look nice when you are all done. This works to make the web page stay formatted correctly and ensures that you are going to get a nice looking web page when it is all done.

- *Margin and padding properties*

Margins and padding inside of your code are going to be transparent. This means that you will not be able to change up the color, but you can have some say in their width. The pixel is the method that is used most of the time to specify the width that you would like to use. For example, if you want to make sure that you are making the margin 10 pixels, you will need to write out "margin: 10px;" to tell the compiler what you would like to see happen. You will be able to do the same thing with padding, just use the syntax that is above and write out padding instead of margin to make it work.

- *Border Properties*

There is the option to set up how big you would like the border to be as well as the radius, style, and color as well. If you would like to be able to set up how thick the border is, you would need to use what is known as the border-width property. This is usually going to be done in pixels. If you would like to make this simple, you can go with the values that are already set up in the program that are thin, medium, and thick. You can also set the border properties yourself if you would like to make them different sizes to work with what you are doing on your page. For example, if you would like to set the border to be 25 pixels, you would just need to type out "border-width: 25px;"

The next thing that you may want to consider working on is the color of the border. You could just leave it alone and let it go to the default, which is a plain color, but if you would like to add some color to the border because it helps you to make the page look better than before, you would be able to go with that. There are 140 predefined colors inside of the CSS option so you will be able to pick out the one that you would like. Some simple colors like yellow, red, and green all are possible. You can also choose to make the border color transparent so that there isn't really a border present inside the code.

Yu can also use the RGB notation in order to get the right tone of color that you want. All of the colors on the web are going to be represented with your three primary colors, which are Red, Green and Blue in the computer world. If you write out rgb (0, 255, 0) this means that you want to have a pure green color. You can have different variants of the number to make sure that you get the shade that you would like.

The hexadecimal notation will use six different digits to represent the color that you would like to use. The first two numbers are going to represent the hexadecimal color for red followed by the ones for green, and then finally the last two are for blue. Each of the colors that you would like to use will use a different number on this system.

Some of the other things that you are able to do with your border include changing the style of the border, such as adding in a groove, a ridge, an inset, or something else to make it look a little bit different as well as adding in some more color to help out. The radius of the border is another thing that you are able to work with. This one is used when you would like to round up the corners a bit and it is going to be used as a percentage and pixel. As long as you write out the corner that you would like to change, you will be able to pick out one or two corners and change those without changing all of them.

Positioning and Floating

Now that we know a bit more about the box model that comes with using CSS, it is time to work with this program in order to specify the arrangement of the boxes and where you would like to place them on the web page. You don't want to have them just randomly show up on the page, rather you want to pick out where you are putting all of the parts on the page to make it stay in order and look at good as possible. In this section, we are going to talk about two important concepts inside of the CSS program, how to work with floating and positioning since both of these are so important to help you handle the layout of your web page.

- *Positioning*

The first thing that we are going to look at is the positioning property. This is the one that will allow you to position an element and then specify which element should be on top in case of any overlapping in what you are working on.

There are four methods that you are able to use when it comes to positioning the element. The first one is the static positioning. This one doesn't mean too much, just that the elements are going to be positioned according to what is seen as the normal flow of the page. All of your HTML elements are going to be positioned using this method by default so if you don't pick out another option, this is the one that the system is going to use. If you want to make sure that the static positioning is the one that is going to be used, such as overriding another positioning rule for the same element, you would need to write out "position: static;"

The next method that you can use for positioning things is the relative positioning method. This method is going to position an element relative to its normal position. This is the default position of your element when there isn't positioning rules or when the static positioning is used. Suppose that you are working with two boxes, such as box1 and box2, and they don't have any positioning specified. If we create box2 after we worked on box1 in HTML, the box2 is going to automatically be positioned under box1 by default. Here is the code for how the original box1 and box 2 would be placed on the page:

```
<!DOCTYPE html>

<html>

<head>

<style>

#box1 {

        /*Some rules for styling box1*/

}

#box2 {

        /*Some rules for styling box2*/

}

</style>

</head>

<body>

<div id-"box1">Box 1</div>

<div id="box2">Box 2</div>

</body>

</html>
```

With this option, the second box is going to show up directly below the first box, and they are going to be lined up together so that you will see one right after the other. This may make sense in some cases depending on how you would like to work on the page, but there may be times when you would like to move the second box around a bit. It is still going to be below the first box, but you are able to move around the second box based on a relative position from where it originally was located. Let's add these into the rules of box2:

position: relative;

left: 150px;

top: 50px;

This is going to allow us to change the location of the box2. We are moving it over to the left by 150 pixels and then down by 50 pixels to give it a new position on the page. You are also able to move it up and to the left as well depending on where you would like to put them. This provides you with some options of where you would like to put all of the boxes based on where they are in the code and can help you to make the page more interesting.

The third method for positioning that you may want to use is the fixed positioning option. As you can guess from this game, you will be able to put an element in the fixed method to keep it at the right assigned location. It is not going to move even when you scroll down the page. This is something that is used often when you want the social sharing buttons to be present on the side of your web page no matter where the user is scrolling. To use the fixed position, you will simply need to write out "position: fixed;"

When we are using the fixed positioning, we are able to use the top property to specify the number of pixels the box should be from the top of the page while the left property is going to specify the number of pixels it should be from the left of the page. In addition to these ones, you can also use the bottom and right properties, which is going to be used in order to specify the number of pixels the box should be from the bottom and the right side of the page.

The nice part about using this one is that it allows you to keep the box moving down as the person scrolls up and down the page. This can make sure that the right information is always present right away for the user and they won't have to look around to find what they want each time.

And finally, the last method of positioning that you may want to use is the one of absolute positioning. When this option is used, an element is going to be positioned relative to the first parent element that has a position other than static. If no such element is found, this one is going to be positioned relative to the page. This one is kind of similar to what you will find with relative positioning, but the element is going to be positioned in a way that is relative to the parent element instead of based on the normal position. (Tutorial Republic)

Floating

The other property that you are able to use inside of CSS is floating. This is a technique that has been used in order to arrange elements onto the page. A good way to think about this is that it is similar to putting books onto a shelf. Think about having a stack of books that are varying in color, height, and thickness and you need to be able to put all the books on the shelf in some way. In addition, you will not be allowed to rearrange the books later on so you need to do it the right way. This means that the books need to be placed onto the bookshelf in the exact order they were in the original stack.

To perform this task in CSS, we will need to start out using the top row. We will need to start putting back onto the top row, one by one and going from left to right. Now you can suppose that the top row is full and you have a book that just is too big to fit on this top row. In most cases, you would move this to the second row and keep on going, but when working with CSS, this is not really the way that things are done. The CSS, this book is still going to be fit into the same row, but maybe a bit below the previous book as long as there is a little bit of space to do this. This method of stacking the books is similar to doing a float: left inside of CSS.

You can also do a float: right, which is when you work on the top row, but you stack books from right to left instead.

Here, we are going to take a look at the code that you would need to use to make this happen. We are going to assume that we have 7div boxes that are of varying heights and widths and we are going to float them left. Here is the code that we need to use:

```
<!DOCTYPE html>

<html>

<head><title>CSS Float</title>

<style type ="text/css">

div {

        padding: 10px;

        border: 1 px dashed black;

        margin: 5px;

float: left;

}

#box1 {

        width: 60px;

        height: 100px;
```

```
}

#box2 {

        Width: 100px;

        Height: 20px;

}

#box3 {

        Width: 50px;

        Height: 150 px;

}

#box4 {

        Width: 20 px;

        Height: 50 px;

}

#box5 {

        Width: 150px;

        Height: 120px;

}
```

```
#box6 {

        Width: 120px;

        Height: 70px;

}

#box7 {

        Width: 25px;

        Height: 80px;

}

</style></head>

<body>

        <div id="box1">Box 1</div>

        <div id="box2">Box 2</div>

        <div id="box3">Box 3</div>

        <div id="box4">Box 4</div>

        <div id="box5">Box 5</div>

        <div id="box6">Box 6</div>

        <div id="box7">Box 7</div>
```

```
</body>

</html>
```

(Riwalk, 2010)

With this code, you would be able to get the first five boxes on the top line, with the fifth box going right under your small fourth box. Then the last two boxes would be moved down to the second shelf of the code. You are able to use as many of these boxes as you would like, but the CSS page is going to be able to choose how many of each box fits into the row and they will keep adding more as long as they fit in the same row.

Display and Visibility

At this point, we have spent some time talking about CSS and all of the different points that come up with this language. We have covered a lot of the important concepts that come with CSS including the box model option, the idea of positioning and floating, and so much more. In this section, we are going to take a look at how to work with visibility and display inside of the CSS program.

- *Display*

The first one of these that we are going to talk about is the display property. This is the one that you will need to use when you want to change how an element is displayed. There are three values that are the most commonly used in this including block, inline, and none. The first value of none has the ability to make some elements disappear. The page is going to show up as if your element is no longer there. There are probably not many times when you would want to use this value.

The second value, or the inline value, is the one that is going to display the element as an inline element. Remember that an inline element does not start and end with a new line like you will see with some of the other options. Another thing that you will notice with the inline element is that it will only take up as much width and height as it needs. You will not have to waste your time trying to specify this in the inline element because it is just going to be big enough to hold the information that you want inside.

And finally, the second element that you may use inside of the display is the block element. This one is going to start as well as end with a new line and both the width and the height can be changed. You will be able to decide how big you would like the display to be based on the amount of information that you have inside of it and how you want it to work on the web page.

- *Visibility*

The property of visibility inside of CSS is often used in order to hide an element. You will be able to use the code "visibility: hidden;" if you would like to hide one of your elements. So how is this different from the display: none that we were talking about before? The difference is with the visibility: hidden, you will still have the element taking up space, you just won't be able to see it. This is kind of like giving the element an invisible clock; it is still there on the page, you just won't be able to see it. When it comes to using the display: none option, the element is taken off the page and your page is going to get rid of it as if the element didn't exist at all.

Both the display and the visibility are important when it comes to working on the different parts of your web page. You are able to use these in order to determine where all of the parts on the page are going to be located, whether you would like them to be lined up in a certain way or even if you would like it if they were invisible to see right from the start. Making sure to learn how to use these properly can make it easier than ever to get the results that you want when using these two parts.

Background

There are a lot of times when you would like to mess around with what you are doing in the background of your page. This can help to make it easier to read the information that is on the web page, ensures that you can add in some colors if you would like to spruce it up, and makes it so that you are able to do a handful of other things to make the page really stand out. The background image and the background color are the two most common things that you will do when it comes to the background of your web page.

- *Background color*

So, the first thing that we are going to take the time to look at is the background color of your web page. You would just need to use the property "background-color" in order to tell the compiler what color you would like to use. You can then choose whether you would like to just name the color you want to use (remember that there are 140 colors that are recognized by CSS), the rgb method, or the hexadecimal method to pick out the color that you want to use. Pick the right method that you want to use and put it with the property discussed above (the "background-color" part) and you will be able to see all the variances that come with different background colors.

- *Background Image*

Now let's say that you would like to do something a little bit different for your background. Rather than just having one solid background there, you would like to put in an image in the background. You are able to pick just one or two large pictures that you would like to have in the background or you can choose to have the picture repeat a few times in the background going all over the place.

If you would like to just have the one image in the background, you would just need to use the code "background-image: url("image1.jpg");" but if you would like to take the image and get it to repeat, starting from the top left corner, and then go all throughout the page both horizontally and vertically. If you want to avoid this, the background-repeat property can help you out with this as well. There are a few different things that you are able to do with this property including the following:

Repeat: this is going to be the default. The image is going to be repeated both vertically and horizontally.

Repeat-x: this is when you just want the image to be repeated going horizontally.

Repeat-y: this is when you only want the image to be repeated vertically.

No-repeat: this is when you don't want the image to be repeated at all.

You can also work with the background attachment feature. This one is going to tell the document whether the picture in the background should scroll along with the page so that the user can see it the whole time that they are on the page or if it should be fixed to just one part. You will be able to use the scroll and fixed keywords to try and keep the picture in the right location.

Navigation bars, links, and lists

In this section, we are going to spend some time looking at the properties that are needed to help with lists and hyperlinks. We will be able to discuss both of these concepts by the end and then discuss how you are able to use this information in order to create the navigation bars that you often see on other web pages. We are going to do this by discussing CSS lists.

- *CSS lists:*

Remember that when working in HTML, we are able to create two types of lists, an unordered list and an ordered list. We are able to style these lists with the help of some of the properties of the CSS list.

The first property that we are going to use is the list-style-type property. This makes it easier for you to set the list item markers for your list. The list item markers are going to refer to the letters, numbers, and bullets that are on the left of each list item. For an ordered list, we are able to specify the type of letters or numbers that we would like to use as our markers. For example, if we want to use roman numbers for our item markers, we would just need to write out the following code "list-style-type: lower-roman;" and then it would be all set up.

Some of the other default or commonly used markers that you are able to choose from include;

Decimal: this is the one that will be the default unless you take the time to specify it.

Decimal-leading-zero: this would be options like 01, 02, 03 and so on.

Lower-alpha:

Lower-greek:

Upper-alpha

Upper-roman:

If you are working on an unordered list, you will be able to specify the shape that you would like to use on the bullet. The default for this is the disc, which is the filled in circle, but you can choose to make this a regular circle or a square. In addition, you can choose to not have any item marker for the list. You would simply put in the none keyword with the list-style-type part and you are set to go.

Next, you can work on the list-style-position property that is used in many cases in order to specify whether the list item markers should be on the outside or the inside of the content flow. You will simply use the keywords, inside or outside, to make this happen. By default, the list items that you will use are going to be displayed with a little bit of indentation. If you use the keyword inside for this, the list item markers are going to be displayed after you do the indentation. The indentation would be represented by the left edge of the boxes. If the keyword outside is used, the markers are going to be shown before the indentation.

The list-style option is a good property to use when you would like to work on the settings for all of the list properties all in one. So, if you would like to make changes to any of the lists that we have talked about so far in this section, you would be able to use the list-style option and get it all done in one line. If any of the values are missing, you will find that the CSS program is just going to use the default value for that missing property. A good example of this is "list-style: square inside url("myMarker.gif");".

- *CSS Links*

Hyperlinks are a great thing to add into your code. They will allow you to point the reader to other pages on your site, to other locations on the page, and even to another website if you chose to give your user that information to help prove a point. There are many times when you will need to add in these hyperlinks. These can be styled using any of the same properties that we have talked about in the previous chapters. In addition to getting to choose to style the hyperlinks based on the state they are in, you can pick from four total states to work with the links including:

- Link: this is a link that has not been visited by the user yet.

- Visited: this is a link that has been clicked on and visited.

- Hover: this is the link and how it will appear when the user hovers right over it.

- Active: this is what happens when the link is clicked.

There is just so much that you are going to be able to do when you are working in the CSS language. You will be able to combine it together with the HTML documents that you are working on to ensure that you are getting the best look on your web page that you are looking for. There are so many people who are looking to create a great website and whether you are doing it on your own or with the help of some online website builder, it is still a good idea to learn how to work with the CSS and HTML documents to understand exactly what you need to do to make your website look amazing.

CHAPTER 7
CSS DO'S AND DON'TS

These are some of the more important Do's and Don'ts for CSS:

CSS and HTML are both key languages to get started on when you decide that you are going to learn web development. They are incredibly powerful and, most of the time, they are relatively easy to work with. However, everyone, beginners and pro's alike, have all made mistakes, be they minor, basic ones or major ones. One of the biggest mistakes is thinking that, because your page looks fine, it is fine. In all truthfulness, you should learn never to trust everything that you have coded. For example, if you used the same ID two or more times on one page won't give you any errors and it won't show you any alignment issues unless of course, you validate it, but it is bad markup practice and it is, to all intents and purposes, a major error.

Use your DOCTYPE

Remember the extra-long DOCTYPES that we once used, the ones that you could never remember? Now, all you need to do at the top of your document is to input <!DOCTYPE HTML>, a much cleaner way of doing things. No excuse for forgetting it, right?

Wrong! So many people still forget to specify their DOCTYPE and, for an HTML document that is organized and will validate correctly, it must be included.

ID vs Classes

ID's are unique identifiers that let you target certain elements. Because they are unique, you may only use one on a page. Classes, however, do the exact opposite and are used when there is one element used several times on a page. Here's how you should NOT do it:

```
[code lang="HTML"]
&lt;div id="block"&gt;
&lt;div id="btn"&gt;&lt;/div&gt;
&lt;div id="btn"&gt;&lt;/div&gt;
&lt;/div&gt;
[/code]
```

And this is how it should be done:

```
[code lang="HTML"]
&lt;div id="block"&gt;
&lt;div class="btn"&gt;&lt;/div&gt;
&lt;div class="btn"&gt;&lt;/div&gt;
&lt;/div&gt;
[/code]
```

Forget Inline Styling

Sadly, this is a common thing and a bad thing. It is not related to bad markup or even invalid code but with the organization and structure of your CSS code. Let's say you have 25 pages and you have an inline style that needs to be removed from the same <div> on every page – how long is that going to take you? Here's is what you should NOT do:

```html
[code lang="html"]
&lt;div style="width: 100%; background: #fff;"&gt;&lt;/div&gt;
[/code]
```

And how it should be done:

```html
[code lang="html"]
&lt;div id="wrap"&gt;&lt;/div&gt;
[/code]
```

Don't overuse the CSS Classes and Divs

You just got started on a project of your own and you learned how to use classes, ID's and divs. Fortunately, you are not into inline styling but you just love to get creative with styles and put them everywhere. That's really great but you should never write more code than you absolutely need to. There really isn't any need to have a div that contains an unordered list with a class that has been applied to every li element. Here's how NOT to do it:

```
[code lang="html"]
&lt;div id="navigation"&gt;
&lt;ul&gt;
&lt;li class="left"&gt;&lt;/li&gt;
&lt;li class="left"&gt;&lt;/li&gt;
&lt;li class="left"&gt;&lt;/li&gt;
&lt;/ul&gt;
&lt;/div&gt;
[/code]
```

And this is how it should be done:

```
[code lang="html"]
&lt;ul id="navigation"&gt;
&lt;li&gt;&lt;/li&gt;
&lt;li&gt;&lt;/li&gt;
&lt;li&gt;&lt;/li&gt;
&lt;/ul&gt;
[/code]
```

And don't forget your stylesheet:

```
[code lang="css"]
#navigation li { float: left; }
[/code]
```

Set Your Browser Resolution Right

Around 10% of Internet users have a resolution of 1024 x 768 on their screen while the rest are on a bigger resolution. When you ask yourself which resolution your website should be designed for, the answer is, everyone. Go for something like a standard 960 px or 980 px for width and somewhere between 550 and 640 px for the horizontal. 10% may be low but it is still representative of millions of users. Your website should be designed for all users.

Block vs Inline elements

Telling the difference between block elements and inline elements is a bit of a sticky subject for some beginners. Block elements are displayed on new lines with a default width of 100% of the element that contains it, such as a <div> or a <p>. The inline elements are displayed without line breaks which means they begin on the same line and have only their own width. You can make a change to how an element is displayed as well so you can have an inline element display like a block and vice versa. Here's how it should be done:

[code lang="css"]

span { display: block; }

[/code]

Always Comment Your Code

When you begin a new project, you should get into the habit of commenting as much as you possibly can. This helps with organization and it can help you locate an element or section that you may be looking for. It will also help you to know which div is being closed by </div>. Here's how it should be done:

How you should do it

```html
[code lang="html"]
&lt;!– Begin #header –&gt;
&lt;div id="header"&gt;
&lt;!– End #header –&gt;
&lt;/div&gt;
[/code]
```

Stylesheet:

```css
[code lang="css"]
/* ––––––––––––––––––––––––
Header
–––––––––––––––––––––––– */
#header { background: #fff; }
[/code]
```

Don't Forget Cross-Browser Compatibility

When you create something, you should always do it from the point of view of the end-user. Some users are still on early versions of Internet Explorer, like version 6 or 7. While that may be years old, not everybody has the hardware capable of running newer versions and not everyone wants to update so you need to take these users into account. A page rendered in Firefox looks completely different in Google Chrome and different again in Internet Explorer. Use online tools to see how your website will render on different browsers and tweak until you get it somewhere near right for all of them.

Keep Things Simple

When you write code, you should always have the future in mind. You already know how to use comments and you manage to keep your code fairly organized but you don't need to stop there. Specify some generic classes and use them with the other elements when you are working on your HTML. Here's how NOT to do it:

Stylesheet

```css
[code lang="css"]
#firstblock { background: #000; float: left; }
.genblock { background: #006699; float: left; }
[/code]
```

HTML

```
[code lang="html"]
&lt;div id="firstblock"&lt;/div&gt;
&lt;div class="genblock"&gt;&lt;/div&gt;
[/code]
```

And how it should be done:

Stylesheet

```
[code lang="css"]
.left { float: left; }
#firstblock { background: #000; }
.genblock { background: #006699; }
[/code]
```

HTML

```
[code lang="html"]
&lt;div id="firstblock" class="left"&gt;&lt;/div&gt;

&lt;div class="genblock left"&gt;&lt;/div&gt;

[/code]
```

This is an easy way to declare two classes and keeping things very organized. Do the same thing with properties – there really isn't any need to keep on writing the same property repeatedly when you could do it just once. Again, here's how NOT to do it:

```css
[code lang="css"]
#content { margin-top: 10px; margin-right: 12px; margin-bottom: 0; margin-left: 15px; background-color: #000; background-repeat: no-repeat; }
[/code]
```

And how it should be done:

```css
[code lang="css"]
#content { margin: 10px 12px 0 15px; background: #000 no-repeat; }
[/code]
```

You and how you work will determine how many CSS files you need in your project but, rather than using tons of different ones, keep it simple and stick to a couple of main generic ones, like reset.css and style.css. At the end of the day, your code must be easy to read and even easier to edit when needed.

Don't Be Random in Your Use of Heading Tags

The heading tags are not there to make your code look good; they are there to establish how important each piece of content is in terms of SEO. There are 6 heading tags – h1 to h6. Obviously, h1 is the top one and it should only be used for the business name or the web page name. use the rest of the tags according to the importance of the titles and content but don't sprinkle them all through your code. Here's how NOT to do it:

[code lang="html"]

<h6>Post title</h6>

<h1>Text content</h1>

[/code]

And hw it should be done:

[code lang="html"]
<h2>Post title</h2>
<p>Text content</p>
[/code]

Only Use Absolute Position When Truly Necessary

Beginners have been known to get addicted to using absolute positioning simply because it is one of the easiest ways to place your elements. However, excessive use of it is not good practice. Elements that have absolute positioning tend to not have a natural flow and that makes it difficult to get them aligned with other page sections. You can't tell a normal element that it has to be on the left-hand side of an element that has an absolute position! Get out of the habit of using it because it's easy and into the habit of using it when necessary.

Type Fonts

Do you have a favorite font and really want to see it on your web page? If so, is it one of the standard ones or a specialized one? When you pick a font, you must always have another as a backup, and another and another if necessary. Not every user has the same fonts as you and if you don't have backups, they won't see what you want them to see. If you want to use a font that is not standard, the easiest way is to use @font-face. Here's how NOT to do it:

```css
[code lang="css"]
p { font-family: AurulentSansRegular, Arial, Helvetica, sans-serif;
}
[/code]
```

And how it should be done:

```css
[code lang="css"]
@font-face {

font-family: 'AurulentSansRegular';

src: url('AurulentSans-Regular-webfont.ttf') format('truetype');

}

p { font-family: 'AurulentSansRegular', Arial, Helvetica, sans-serif; }
```

[/code]

Constantly Validate

This one's self-explanatory. You must constantly validate your work as you go along. This will make it easier for you to see where you are going wrong and raise your chances of having a near perfect web page when you are done. There are two tools that you can use – HTML Validator and CSS Validator. Get into the habit of using them regularly.

CHAPTER 8
LEARNING JAVASCRIPT: MAKING THE WEB MORE INTERACTIVE

So far, you have learned how to create a basic web page with HTML. You also know how to make your web pages look beautiful with the help of CSS. However, that is not really enough for a modern web page. These days, a website needs to be interactive. In order to do so, you need to implement JavaScript.

What is JavaScript?

JavaScript is actually a dynamic programming language. When used alongside HTML, it can provide the web page with dynamic interactivity. However, JavaScript, or JS for short, is mainly used as a scripting language in an HTML document. This language does not require constant downloads and can be run easily. It is commonly used for quizzes and polls.

Understanding Scripting Language

Before we learn all about JavaScript we need to understand what a script is. It is a sequence of statements which provide instructions for certain tasks to be performed. Generally, scripting languages are easier to learn and faster to code than structured languages. Few other examples of scripting languages are; Python, PHP, Tcl etc. These languages can be rooted within HTML and are typically used to add functionality to the web page such as graphic displays or different menu styles. Scripting languages can be client side or server side. Under client side scripting languages, the data that the end user sees is affected whereas in the server side scripting language the data is manipulated in a database on the server.

JavaScript can be used for providing responses to the users or even to start a slideshow. With a scripting language like JavaScript, a basic web page can be turned into a lively platform for the users.

History of JavaScript

JavaScript was created in the year 1995 for use in a web browser, Netscape Navigator. The original name of this language was Mocha, which was given by the founder of Netscape, Marc Andreessen. Later in that year, the name was changed to LiveScript and after receiving a trademark license, the name JavaScript was given. The first trademark version of the language was released in the year 1997 under the name ECMAScript.

Today JavaScript has entered a completely new phase of evolution. There has been a lot of innovations, standardizations and new developments according to the modern day browsers.

Features of JavaScript

1. **Browser Support**- Most of the browser accepts this scripting language and hence no additional plugins are needed.

2. **Can be used on both server side and client side**- The user can actually change the structure of web pages at runtime since JavaScript has access to the DOM (document object model). Hence, it can be used to add different effects to the web pages. Also, it can be used on the server side as well.

3. **Functional programming language**- in this language a function can be assigned to variables just like any other data types. Apart from that, a function can accept another function as a parameter.

4. **Support for object**s-It is an object oriented language which makes it easy to learn and use.

5. **Large library to work with**: you are going to enjoy that the JavaScript language comes with a large library that you are able to work with on your own. As a beginner, you are able to go through this and see how to work with the codes without having to make up and create as many as you would think for your projects.

6. **A big community**: as a beginner, you are sure to have a lot of questions and concerns about how to create one of your own

codes in this language. There is a large community that you will be able to work with inside of this language. You can ask your questions, watch tutorials, and find out everything that you need to get this language started.

7. Other features –

a) It is a case sensitive scripting language

b) It can display information or pull out correct data according to the computer's clock time.

c) It can open pages in customized windows, where you can specify if the menu line, browser buttons, status line or anything else should be present.

d) The content can be displayed randomly without using server programs.

e) All statements in JavaScript are terminated with a semicolon.

Advantages Offered by JavaScript

JavaScript is the most versatile yet simple and effective language. As we have learned about is a wide range of usage and extended functionality now we will look at some of the advantages which are offered by this language. JavaScript offers a range of benefits to the users. Some of them are given below.

1. **Simplicity:** JavaScript, like HTML and CSS, is quite easy to learn. Moreover, you can also start implementing JavaScript code with equal ease. Its syntax is as simple and is close to writing the English language. JavaScript uses the DOM model which has many pre-written functionalities for various objects on pages. Hence, it becomes very easy to develop a script for a custom purpose.

2. **Speed:** JavaScript is executed on the client-side. As a result, all code functions can be executed immediately. There is no need to contact the server and then wait for a response. This allows JavaScript to be quite fast.

3. **Versatility:** JavaScript is compatibility with quite a few other languages. It is, in fact, possible to insert JavaScript into any web page irrespective of its file extension. You can also use JavaScript inside scripts that have been written in PHP, Perl and other languages. Therefore, JavaScript can be used in a wide range of applications.

4. **API Availability:** The availability of Application Programming Interfaces, or APIs for short, provides JavaScript with a range of functionality. This includes the setting of CSS styles, generation of audio samples and dynamic creation of HTML among others. While these APIs are built into the different web browsers, third-party APIs are also

available which allow you to incorporate functionality from other web properties such as social networks like Facebook.

5. **Extended functionality-** JavaScript has third party add-ons like Greasemonkey. This add-on enables developers to write snippets of the language which can execute on the desired page so as to extend its functionality. (Shabeena, 2016) For example, you want to add a feature to a website, you can write it on your own and use this add-on to implement on the web page.

Disadvantages of JavaScript

Theoretically, this language is quite beneficial for developers, but in practicality, it has some disadvantages-

1. Security —Once the snippets written in JavaScript are appended on to the web pages are executed on client's server immediately and hence they might be used to take undue advantage of the user's system. There are certain restrictions which have been set according to modern web standards on browsers. However, malicious code can still be executed.

2. Inconsistency- JavaScript may be rendered differently by different layout engines resulting in inconsistency in terms of interface and functionality. However, the latest versions of JavaScript have been geared according to universal standards but certain variations are still there.

3. Slow execution- Complex scripts in the language take longer starting and running time.

What Can Be Done with JavaScript?

Since its inception JavaScript has been soaring popularity amongst the web developers since a lot of things can be done with JavaScript. In fact, the options are pretty much limitless. It can be used for making simple things such as image galleries, carousels, and providing responses to the button clicks of the user. Advanced features possible with include animated 3D graphics and games. You can even use JavaScript for developing complete database-based apps among other things. Apart from these, there are more modern day uses of JavaScript which we have summarized for you:-

1. It enhances the interfaces HTML gives us. JavaScript converts the normal input box into a combo box where you can enter your own values or choose from a list of preset values.

2. JavaScript can be used to animate elements on a page. For example, highlighting specific sections of a page or to show and hide information can be done easily, thus giving a rich user experience.

3. The layout issues can be fixed with JavaScript. By using this scripting language, one can find area and position of any element on a particular page along with the dimension of the

browser window. This can prevent the overlapping issues. For example, your website has several levels of menu, but upon checking you find out that there is a space for sub-menu. So, by showing it before you can prevent overlapping menu items.

4. Under JavaScript, you can load information which can be accessed by only those users who find it relevant. For example; a navigation menu of a website has 5 links but other links to deeper pages will only be displayed when the user activates the menu item.

5. Information which changes constantly, such as sports match scores or the stock market, can be loaded from time to time without user interaction.

Writing some code in JavaScript

Now that you have JavaScript on your computer, it is time to get started on writing your first code. We will start off with some simple commands before moving on to some that are a bit more complex later on.

As a beginner, you may be worried about how you will start writing out the codes. You may have seen some codes before and feel like they are too impossible to start working on or that since you are not able to read them right now, how are you going to be able to get out there and write some of your own. Luckily, the JavaScript language, as well as many of the other languages for coding out there, have made some changes to ensure that writing and reading codes can be easier than before. By the time you are done, you will find that writing out your own codes in JavaScript is much better.

When it comes to JavaScript, it is important to remember that you are working in a slightly different form of coding, the HTML form, rather than for making games or the other versions offered with options like Python or C++. Because you are working with an HTML language, you will need to make sure that you are using tags and that they are located in the right place inside the language. These tags are going to vary based on what you are trying to get the code to accomplish, but they will follow the same syntax to tell your compiler what actions to take.

The basic syntax of using these codes is <script> and then at the end, it would be </script> (keep in mind that the word script can be replaced with other things based on the different commands that you are trying to give to the coding language. Just remember that the slash mark is important if you would like to be able to end the code that you are writing, and that the portion that doesn't have the slash is going to be how you begin the whole thing. Let's take a look at how this works for writing code and how you will be able to make it work for your needs.

The nice thing about this syntax is that you can use it no matter which command you send to the compiler. You can use it for the

HTML code, for the functions and methods, and anything else you would like to tell the compiler to do. When writing out your syntax, make sure to include the right script codes at the beginning and the end of each code, otherwise the system will return an error to you. Before we move on, let's look at what in-browser JavaScript can do.

Modern JavaScript is seen as a very safe language for programming. Because it was originally created for browsers that do not need low-level access to the CPU or to the memory, it doesn't provide it. Its capabilities will depend almost entirely on what environment JavaScript is being run in. For example, NodeJS will provide support for all functions that let JavaScript read and/or write arbitrary files, perform requests on the network and so on.

In-browser JavaScript is able to do anything that relates to manipulation of web pages, or interaction with the web server and the user. It can:

- Modify styles

- Change content

- Add new HTML

- React to actions from a user

- Run on clicks from a mouse, a key press or a pointer movement

- Send requests to remote servers over the internet

- Download and upload files

- Get cookies and set cookies

- Show messages

- Ask visitors questions

- Remember the client-side data

There are, however, some things that in-browser JavaScript cannot do and this is because the browser abilities are limited for the safety of the user. The reasoning here is to stop evil web pages from getting hold of confidential information and from harming the data of any user. Examples of these restrictions include:

- In-browser JavaScript may NOT read or write arbitrary files to the hard drive, it may not copy them nor may it execute any program. It does not have any direct access to the system functions of the operating system.

- It can work with files in modern browsers but it has limited access. This access will only be provided if a user does a specific action

- The camera, the microphone and other devices may be interacted with but only if the user provides express permission. As such, web pages that are JavaScript enabled, cannot enable web cameras, look at the users' surroundings and send that information off to the NSA without the knowledge and permission of that user.

- Different windows or tabs usually have no idea that there are any others open. The only time they will be aware is when one window or tab uses JavaScript to open another window or tab. Even then, the JavaScript on one may not be able to access the JavaScript in another, especially if they are from different domains, ports or protocols. This is known as 'Same Origin Policy' and to get around it, both of the open pages must have a special JavaScript code that can handle the exchange of data.

Again, this is in place to safeguard the user and stop information from one page being stolen by another. JavaScript is easily able to communicate over the internet to the server for the current page but it is limited or even crippled when it comes to receiving data from those other sites or domains. Although it can be done, it does require an explicit agreement, which must be in the HTML headers, from the remote server.

Writing my code

Understanding what is going on above may seem a bit confusing when you first start, so this section is going to take some more time to look at how it should all work together. We will show an example of a code inside of the JavaScript language so take a bit of time to look at how it is outlined, what parts are present, and more so you can start to see how some of your coding will look when it is your turn to start writing some.

```
<!DOCTYPE html>

<html>

<head>

<meta charset- "ISO-8859-1">

<title> My First JavaScript Program </title>

</head>

<body>

        <script language = "javascript"

type = "text/javascript">

        document.write("Welcome to JavaScript First Program");

        </script>

</body>

</html>
```

As a beginner, this code may not make much sense so let's break it down and learn what it all means.

- *What does this code mean?*

The first part of this code tells the compiler you are working with JavaScript. Some newer versions won't need this part, but other versions need to you to explain which code you are using. The rest lists out what the compiler should provide to your user.

So, when the client uploads the web page where this code is located, they are going to get the message "Welcome to JavaScript First Program." This is the output of the code and it is what the computer is going to put up for the user to see. You are able to change up or modify this saying in any way that you want to have it work on the web page, but for now, we will keep it simple.

- *White space*

When it comes to working on a coding language, you always need to be careful about the white spaces that are present. This can include the white spaces between the words that you write out or it is the line spaces to separate things out. Each coding language is going to read these white spaces in a different manner. Some will see them and assume that they mean something important so you need to be really careful about what you are writing out and how much space you leave between them. Others won't see this difference and allows you some freedom with the spacing because it makes the code much easier to read.

When you are working on JavaScript, the spaces and the line breaks are not as critical as you will find with some of the other coding languages. They are more there to help make the code easy to read and work with, but you could go without them and just write out your whole code on one line. Most programmers like to add in a bit of extra white space because it makes the code a bit easier on the eyes to read. Separating out the different parts of your code with new lines and white spaces makes it easier for other programmers to see how the code works.

- *Using the semicolon*

Another thing that you may have noticed in the code above is that there are some semicolons at the end of parts. You will often find that it is located after the statement has been written out, but it is more an idea of good practice between programmers rather than something that will determine whether the program is going to work in the compiler or not. You should add it in after the statements are done, but if you happen to forget, the compiler is still going to give you all the execution that you are looking for.

- *Case sensitivity*

There are two patterns that can come up when dealing with case sensitivity in your code. Some of the language will notice that there are differences between the upper case and your lower case letters. These languages will read the words Book and book as two separate things. Other languages will be able to see Book and book and think they are the same. When it comes to the

JavaScript language, you are going to have to be careful about the case sensitivity that you are working with. Make sure that you pay attention because if you type in the wrong one with your functions, you will find that it is almost impossible to find that one later on. Always double check which case you are planning on using and then stick with that.

- *Comments*

Comments are another important thing that you can work on when you are writing out your code. These are going to help you to explain what is going on inside of your program without having the compiler make a mess within the system. If you would like to explain what you want the different parts of the code to work on, you would just need to add in certain symbols to make it happen. The programmers who look at your code will be able to look through the comments and see your notes, but the compiler will see the symbols and will just skip right over them to another part.

The nice part is that you are allowed to have as many of these comments inside of your code as you would like. You should use the comments sparingly because using too many could convolute the system and make it harder to read. But if a certain part of the code needs to be explained, don't be afraid to add in one or two of the comments to help.

Putting all of these parts together inside of your code can make it easier than ever to get the results that you want. They all work together, along with some of the information about JavaScript that you will see in the following chapter, in order to make some great codes and ensure that you get the right stuff put on your web page.

CHAPTER 9
FUNDAMENTALS OF JAVASCRIPT

JavaScript has become one of the most prominent languages on the internet. It can be used across platforms and various browsers. Therefore, in order to use this language in the practical world, we need to first learn about its fundamentals. This would give you a foundational understanding of JavaScript.

1. Variables

As you already know, variables are containers in which data can be stored. The data stored in a variable can be an expression or a value. Expressions can be of three types in JavaScript language.

Expression	Description
Logical	Evaluates to a Boolean i.e. true or false
Arithmetic	Evaluates to a number
String	Evaluates to a String

The Scope of Variables in JavaScript

The variable scope refers to the section of the program in which the variable is defined. Variables in JavaScript can have either one of two scopes.

Global Variables: These variables can be defined anywhere in your code due to its global scope.

Local Variables: These variables exist only inside the function that it has been defined in. Function parameters will always be local to that specific function.

The local variable can be declared by using the *var* as keyword and global variables should be used without using *var* as a keyword. For example: If a local variable is declared inside a function and it cannot be accessed outside of that function, thus making it local to that function. In case you declare the same variable without keyword *var*, it becomes accessible to the entire script and not only within that function.

In JavaScript, a local variable will be given precedence inside the body of the function if there is a global variable that has the same name. By declaring a local variable that has the same name as that of a global variable, you are effectively hiding that global variable in the function.

Let us look at an example for a local variable

var num= 20;

If you want to access the value of the num variable at some other point in the script, then you simply refer with the variable name. document.write function writes data to the web page.

Look at the syntax below:

document.write("The value of num is: " +num);

The result which we will get would be "The value of num is 20".

In order to store arithmetic expressions in a variable, we simply need to assign the variable to the calculated value. Not the calculation but the result of that calculation gets stored in that variable. Therefore, once again we will get the result as "The value of num is 20". Look at the following example:

var num = (10+10);

document.write(" The value of num is: "+ num);

In case you want to change the value of a variable then refer to the variable by the name which has been assigned to it and then assign it a new value by using an equal sign. The only difference is that you don't have to use keyword *var* since the variable has already been declared.

var num =20

document.write("The value of num is: " +num);

//update the value of num to 30

num=30;

document.write(" The new value of num is: "+ num);

So, the result for this script would be "The value of num is 20" followed by "The new value of num is 30"

Here is one more example for variable to understand the concept better.

<script type="text/javascript">

<!--

     Var money;

     Var name;

     //-->

</script>

In the above example, the var keyword has been used twice for declaring two variables, money, and name. However, JavaScript allows multiple variables to be declared with just one var keyword. You can see this happening in the following example.

<script type="text/javascript">

<!--

Var money, name;

```
//-->
```

</script>

Variable initialization takes place when a value is stored in a variable. It is possible to perform variable initialization while declaring the variable in JavaScript. Alternatively, you can initialize the variable later when you require that variable. You can see this happening in the following example.

<script type="text/javascript">

<!--

Var name = "John";

Var money;

Money = 12.30;

```
//-->
```

</script>

When using variables, there are two things that you need to keep in mind.

- The *var* keyword must be used either for declaration or initialization. As such, it will be used only once in the lifespan of any variable in a single program. The same variable must never be declared twice, or it can result in errors.

- As JavaScript is an untied language, a variable can hold any value irrespective of the data type. In other words, you do not have to mention what kind of value that a variable should contain while it is being declared. You can change the value type of the variable during the execution. JavaScript will handle it automatically.

Rules for Variable Names

When you are giving names to your variables, you need to remember the following rules.

- All JavaScript variables are identified with unique names and they are called as identifiers. These can be short names, like a and b, or more descriptive names such as sum, age, total volume etc.

- The reserved keywords in JavaScript cannot be used as names for your variables.

- Variable names cannot start with a number in JavaScript. They must either start with a letter or underscore.

- The names can also begin with a $ sign.

- As mentioned earlier, JavaScript is case sensitive. Therefore, the variable names must be used accordingly.

Apart from all the reserved words, there are certain words which cannot be used as JavaScript functions, variables, loop labels, methods or any object names. Listed below are a few of them:

Abstract	Boolean	Break	Switch	Else
Extends	Long	Interface	throw	This
Byte	False	Case	New	null
Class	Final	with	True	float

2. Data types

As you may already know, data types denote the kind of values that can be used in a programming language. There are two kinds of data types in Java Script:

a) Primitive

b) Non-primitive

It is dynamic type language; this means that you don't need to specify the type of variable because it is used dynamically by

JavaScript engine. Here, you need to use *var* to specify the data type.

In JavaScript, there is no difference between floating-point values and integer values. Instead, all numbers are considered to be floating-point values in JavaScript.

Primitive Data Types-They are of five types:

(1) String- this type represents the sequence of characters

(2) Boolean- it represents value as either true or false

(3) Number- it represents the numeric value

(4) Undefined- as the name suggests, it shows the undefined values

(5) Null- represents no value at all.

Nonprimitive data types-

(1) Array- which is group of similar values

(2) Object- represents instance by which we can access members

(3) RegExp- reflects regular expression

Let us look into details of data types:

Arrays- They are almost similar to variables except that they can hold multiple expressions and values under one name and thus making them a powerful data type. There is no limit to the amount of data that can be stored in arrays as long as it is within the scope. One can access any value of any item and any given point of time provided that it is declared in the script. A similar type of data can be stored in one single array and that particular array can be assigned a name which is related to the items it consists of. (Hadlock, 2011)

Let us look at an example:

var shapes = new Array("rectangle", "square", "triangle");

var colors = new Array("red", "pink", "orange");

To access any item in the array you have to use its ID. It is the item's position in the array. Arrays always start with a 0 as an ID instead of 1 which might get confusing in the beginning but with practice you can find the concept easy to learn. The ID's work in ascending order; like 0,1,2,3 and so on. Below is an example to understand this concept-

var colors = new Array("red", "pink", "green");

document.write("red: "+colors[0]);

document.write("pink: "+colors[1]);

document.write("green: "+colors[2]);

In an array, you can also assign values to a particular position. For example:

var colors = new Array ();

colors [0] = "red";

colors [1] = "pink";

colors [2] = "green";

document.write ("pink: "+colors [2]);

//update pink to blue

Colors [1] = "blue";

document.write ("blue: "+ colors [2]);

Objects- The objects are written with curly brackets. The properties of an object are written as –:

name: value pairs, separated by commas

Example for objects:

Var person = {first name: "Ryan", last name: "Booth", age:35, eyeColor: "brown"};

The above example has four properties; age, eye color, first name and last name.

3. **Operators** – To perform any operation in JavaScript we need operators. They include comparison, subtraction, addition and many more. There are four basic operators:

- Assignment

- Arithmetic

- Logical

- Comparison

a) Arithmetic operators-These operators perform basic mathematical operations like division, addition, multiplication, subtraction and so on.

Operator	Description
*	Multiplication
-	Subtraction
+	Addition
/	division
%	To find the remainder (modulus)
--	Decrement
++	increment

b) Assignment Operators-They are used to assign values to variables in JavaScript. Listed below are all available assignment operators:

Operator	Description
=	Equal
+=	Variable is assigned addition value
-=	Variable is assigned subtraction value
*=	Variable is assigned multiplication value
/=	Variable is assigned division value
%=	Variable is assigned modulo value

Example: var num =20;

document.write("The value of num is: "+num);

//update the value of num to 30

num= (num+10);

document.write(" The new value of num is: "+num);

c) Comparison Operators- These operators establish the relationship between variables or their values. They are used inside conditional statements (we will learn about this later) to create logic by comparing variables or their values. This helps in evaluating whether the statement is true or false. Types of comparison operators are:

Operator	Description
<	Less than
>	Greater than
==	Equal to
!=	Not equal to
===	Equal to, in object and value type
>=	Greater than or equal to
<=	Less than or equal to

(Hadlock, 2011)

d) Logical Operators- They combine comparison operators and are typically used in conditional statements. Types of Logical operators are:

228

Operator	Description
!	Not
&&	And
||	Or

4. Conditional Statements

Like other programming languages, there are different kinds of conditional statements available in JavaScript. They allow you to define a condition whose results determine the action that will be done. They allow your program to make a decision based on the outcome of the condition and perform the relevant action.

In order to create any kind of logic in a programming language, conditional statements act as the basis for it. Conditional statements can be written in four ways under JavaScript.-

Statement	description
Switch	To execute one out of many scripts
If	Execute a script if a result of a specific condition is true
If..else	There are two codes in this conditional statement. If statement executes a script when the condition is true whereas the code under else statement is executed when the condition is false
If..else if..else	Execute a script if one of the unlimited conditions is true or if all conditions are false then execute another script.

(Hadlock, 2011)

The basic syntax for the if...else statement is given below.

If (expression) {

  Statement(s) to be executed if expression is true

}

Examples:

(a)If

```
var num=20;

if (num==10)

{

document.write( "num is equal to 10");

}
```

(b)   if..else

```
var num= 20;

if (num==10)

{

        Document.write("num is equal to 10");

}

Else

{

        Document.write( "num is NOT equal to 10, num is:
"+num);

}
```

(c) if..else if...else

```
Var num=20;

If (num==10)

{

document.write( "num is equal to 10");

}

else if (num==20)

{

document.write( "num is equal to 20");

}

else

{

document.write( "num is: "+num");

}
```

(d) switch

```
var num= 20;
```

```
switch (num)

{

  case 10:

      document.write(" num is equal to 10");

      break;

  case 20:

      Document.write(" num is equal to 20");

      break;

  default:

      document.write( "num is: "+num);

}
```

(Hadlock, 2011)

In the above example case clause defines whether the value of data used is equal to value of switch and the break statement stops the switch statement from executing the rest of the statement. The default clause identifies a default script if none of the case statements are executed or if break statements are not there in the executed statements. For example

var num=20;

```
switch(num)

{

case 10:

document.write("num is equal to 10");

Break;

case 20:

document.write("num is equal to 20");

default:

document.write("num is: "+num);

}
```

Therefore, the result of above example would be "num is equal to 20" followed by "num is:20"

5) Functions

Functions are the containers for the script. They are only to be executed by a call to the function or an event. Hence, they are not executed when the browser is initially loaded and executes the script that is the part of web page.

For structuring a function, *function* word followed by a space is used. The name of the function can be anything; however, one should ensure that the name given is related to the task it will perform. Example:

```
var num =20;

function changevariablevalue()

{

        num=21;
}

Changevariablevalue();

Document.write( "num is: "+num);
```

6) Loops

Loops are used to iterate the arrays and execute script along while accessing their values. Loop typically consists of the variable that has been assigned a numeric value. That variable is then used with a comparison operator to compare it against other value. After this, the numeric value is increased or decreased. The comparison in the loop typically determines whether the initial value of a variable is greater or less than another numeric value. So, until the time that condition is true, the loop will run and the value of the variable is increased or decreased till the time condition becomes false.

Looping allows you to execute a single block of code multiple times till a given condition is met. JavaScript offers two kinds of loops, the for loop, and the while loop.

a) The for loop

The for loop allows the same block of code statements to be repeatedly executed till a certain specified condition is met. The syntax of the for loop is given as follows.

For (initial expression; condition expression; loop expression)

{Statements}

Example:

var colors = new array("red", "pink", "green");

for var (i=0; i<colors.length; i++)

{

Document.write("The color is: "+ colors[i] +
);

}

The above example shows a for loop that runs till the time numeric value is less than the length of the array.

b) The while loop

With the while loop, it becomes possible to control the number of times the loop is executed. In other words, this loop is used when you know the number of times a loop needs to be executed. As such, you need to make sure that loop is written properly so that it does not get repeated infinitely. The syntax of the while loop is given below.

While (expression) {

Statement(s) to be executed if expression is true

}

Example:

var i =0;

while (i<10)

{

document.write(i + "<br/>");

i++:

}

In the above example script in this type of loop includes a line that repeats the numeric value until the condition in while loop is false. So, if this line is not there then it will be an endless loop.

The Hello World Example in JavaScript

Here is the hello world example in JavaScript. This will illustrate how the language works and familiarize you with the syntax as well. As you will see, the language is quite simple.

```
<Html>

<Body>

<script language="javascript" type="text/javascript">

<!--

   document.write ("Hello World!")

   //-->

</script>

</body>

</html>
```

The Syntax in JavaScript

JavaScript is supposed to be implemented with the help of JavaScript statements. These statements are placed inside the <script>... </script> HTML tags in a web page. The <script> tags can be placed anywhere within the HTML document. The <script> tag will alert the browser to interpret the text between the tags as a script. An example of the JavaScript syntax is given below.

<script language="javascript" type="text/javascript">

Code in JavaScript

</script>

The script tag has two crucial attributes. They are given below.

1. **Language:** This attribute is used to specify which scripting language is being used. Of course, since you are using JavaScript, the value of this attribute is javascript. On the other hand, this attribute is rarely used these days for the recent versions of HTML and XHTML.

2. **Type:** This attribute is now currently being used for indicating the scripting language. The value of this attribute should be set as 'text/javascript.'

Line Breaks and White space

JavaScript will ignore white spaces. Therefore, you use newlines, tabs, and spaces in your scripts freely. Of course, you should be using them to format your programs and make them look consistent and neat. This allows the code to be read and understood easily.

Semicolons

Generally, semicolons are used to mark the end of statements. This is the case in languages like Java, C++, and C. However, JavaScript makes semi colons optional in one condition. You need to ensure that each statement has been placed on a separate line. As long as you meet this condition, you can avoid inserting semicolons in the code. However, using semicolons is a good practice especially when you are learning to program.

Case Sensitivity

You need to ensure the proper uses of cases in JavaScript as this language is case-sensitive. Therefore, all keywords, function names, variables and other identifiers must be typed with the correct case. Consistency is vital. In JavaScript, the identifiers hi and HI will have different meanings.

How to Place JavaScript in HTML Documents?

One of the good things about JavaScript is that you have the flexibility to add the code anywhere you want in an HTML document. Nonetheless, it is an excellent idea to follow the preferred methods. This can improve the readability and execution of the JavaScript code in the HTML document. Here are the best ways to include JavaScript in HTML.

Inside the <head> tags

This option is generally used when you want the script to run when an event takes place. For example, you may want the script to run when the user clicks something somewhere. In these situations, the script will be placed inside the <head> tags as shown in the following example.

<Html>

<Head>

<script type="text/javascript">

<!--

    Function sayHello () {

    Alert ("Hello World")

    }

    //-->

</script>

</head>

<Body>

<input type="button" onclick="sayHello ()" value="Say Hello" />

</body>

```
</html>
```

1. Inside the <body> tags

In some cases, you may need the script to run while the page loads. This is done to allow the script to generate the content located in the page. In this case, the script will have to be placed inside the <body> tags. In this method, you will not have any function that has been defined with JavaScript. You can see the example given below for such an inclusion of JavaScript.

```
<Html>

<Head>

</head>

<Body>

<script type="text/javascript">

<!--

    document.write ("Hello World")

    //-->

</script>
```

```
<p>Web Page Body </p>

</body>

</html>
```

2. Inside the <head> and <body> tags

If you want, you can combine the two methods above. In other words, you can place your JavaScript code inside both, the <head> and the <body> tags, in the same document. Check out the example given below to see how it works.

```
<Html>

<Head>

<script type="text/javascript">

<!--

    Function sayHello () {

    Alert ("Hello World")

    }

    //-->

</script>

</head>

<Body>
```

```
<script type="text/javascript">

<!--

   document.write ("Hello World")

   //-->

</script>

<input type="button" onclick="sayHello ()" value="Say Hello" />

</body>

</html>
```

3. Inside an External File

Including JavaScript inside the HTML document is a good idea when you are creating simple web pages. However, as you create websites or complex web pages, it is possible that you can find yourself reusing the same JavaScript code in multiple locations. You may even end up using the same code in multiple web pages.

As you have seen in CSS, it is possible for you to create an entirely separate file to keep your JavaScript code. You can put in all the JavaScript code that needs to be used in multiple locations or web pages inside an external file. That file should have the '.js.' extension and be associated with the web pages that require the code. The following example illustrates how an external JavaScript file can be included in an HTML document. In this example, filename.js is the file used for containing the JavaScript code.

```
<Html>

<Head>

<script type="text/javascript" src="filename.js" ></script>

</head>

<Body>

    .......

</body>

</html>
```

Events in JavaScript

An event is an action that causes a JavaScript code to be executed. Events are generally triggered by the users. For example, the click of a mouse can be an event. Based on the events, it is possible to code a response in JavaScript. For example, displaying a message can be a response to an event. These responses can be said to be the event handlers as they handle the event taking place. In JavaScript, it is possible to classify events in a number of ways. After all, there are a huge number of them.

1. The onClick event

The most common event type is the onClick event. This takes place whenever the user left-clicks the web page. Against this event, you can make the appropriate response such as displaying a message or putting your validation. The following example illustrates the use of such an event for displaying a message.

```html
<Html>

<Head>

<script type="text/javascript">

<!--

    Function sayHello () {

    Alert ("Hello World")

    }

    //-->

</script>

</head>

<Body>

<p>Click the following button and see result</p>

<Form>
```

```
<input type="button" onclick="sayHello ()" value="Say Hello" />
```

```
</form>
```

```
</body>
```

```
</html>
```

2. onSubmit Event type

This type of event occurs when a form is submitted. The form validation can be put against this event. Let us look at an example-

If the validate() function in the below mentioned example returns true then only the form will get submitted, if not that than the form will not be submitted.

```
<html>

    <head>

    <script type= "text/javascript">

    <!—

    function validation() {

    all validation goes here

    .......

    return either true or false
```

```
        }

        //-- >

        </script>

</head>

<body>

        <form method= "post" action= "t.cgi" onsubmit= "return
validate()">

        .......

        <input type "submit" value= "Submit"/>

</form>

</body>

</html>
```

(Tutorials Point)

3. onmouseover and onmouseout

This event gives a nice effect both with images and text. When you
bring your mouse over an element onmouseover event is triggered
and when the mouse is moved out then onmouseout is triggered.
Example:

```
<html>
```

```
<head>

<script type= "text/javascript">

<!—

function over () {

document.write ( "mouse over");

}

function out() {

document.write ( "mouse out");

}

//-- >

</script>

</head>

<body>

        <p> drag your mouse inside the division to view the
result:</p>

        <div onmouseover= "over ()" onmouseout="out()">

        <h2> It is inside the division </h2>

        </div>
```

```
</body>

</html>
```

(Tutorials Point)

Some tips for using JavaScript

1. Ensure that JavaScript aids the user in reaching a goal efficiently and quickly. In case it doesn't that means that you are probably using it wrong.

2. The JavaScript solutions that you provide to the user should be naturally better than the earlier interaction. However, the solution should not be so different that the user is not able to relate to it with previous experience. The aim is to ensure that end user feels satisfied with the solution.

3. In case you are handling sensitive data, do not rely on JavaScript since all codes are easily available to read. Apart from that users might turn off JavaScript in their browsers.

We can say that there are so many possibilities with this simple but rich scripting language. JavaScript provides the tools that allow the end users to interact with a web page after it has been downloaded. In this chapter, we have learned fundamentals of JavaScript, now let us look at some frequently asked questions about this programming language.

FAQ's

1. Is JavaScript same as Java?

Answer: No, they are different programming languages. Java is a general purpose programming language, whereas JavaScript is used to make websites more interactive.

2. What all browsers support JavaScript?

Answer: JavaScript is supported by most of the browsers. Listing some of them

- Microsoft Internet Explorer version 3.0 and above

- Netscape Navigator version 2.0 and above

- Safari

- Firefox

- Safari

- Google Chrome

- Opera

3. How can we add a comment in JavaScript?

Answer: Three different types of comments are supported by JavaScript

a) Multiple line C-Style comments, where everything written between /*and*/ is a comment

b) Online comments of C++ style. The comments under this type begin with // and continue till the next line break.

c) HTML style comments begin with (<!--)

4. Can a warning be displayed for the user in case the user is is unable to execute the JavaScript code?

Answer: Yes, a warning can be displayed to the user about the JavaScript incapable browsers. The warning text can be placed between the tags <NOSCRIPT> and </NOSCRIPT>.

Therefore, the browsers which are JavaScript enabled will ignore everything between these tags and the browsers which cannot execute will display your message on the page. The message will be displayed to users who have disabled JavaScript and to those as well whose browsers do not support JavaScript.

5. Is it possible to delete a JavaScript?

Answer: You cannot always delete JavaScript variable, it depends on the following conditions:

a) JavaScript variable cannot be deleted if it has been declared with keyword *var x;* at the first time. However, as a workaround, a variable can be set to *null* or to *undefined*. But this is not equal to deleting the variable.

b) In case the variable *x* appeared first in the script without any declaration, then the delete operator, i.e. *delete x* can be used.

6. What cannot be done with JavaScript programs?

Answer: The following cannot be done with JavaScript code:

a) Printers or other devices cannot be used on client side LAN or the user's system.

b) Accessing files directly on the user's system or client side LAN. The only exception is the cookie files.

c) Implementing of multithreading or multiprocessing is also not possible.

7. What is a method to delete an array element?

Answer: There are two different ways to delete an array element in JavaScript, they are:

a) myArray.splice(n,1). This is a slower method but does not leave a gap in the array.

b) delete myArray[n] . This method is faster but it leaves a gap in index n.

8. Is there a way to find out that whether the user clicked right or left mouse button? Can *onclick* event handler be used?

Answer: For the left mouse button, the click event is fired. However, depending upon the browser, click may or may not occur in the case of the right mouse button. Especially in Microsoft Internet Explorer click event doesn't work for right mouse button. Therefore, *onclick* event handler is not a reliable method to do right vs left mouse button test. Instead, we should use the *mousedown* events. Most of the browsers support *mouseup* and *mousedown* events for any mouse button.

9. What kind of number formatting can be used in JavaScript?

Answer: Mathematical constants and number literals can be written in many ways under JavaScript code, such as:

a) Decimal numbers in exponential form, e.g.: 5.57e-11

b) Conventional decimal numbers, e.g. : 5, 7, 137 , 1.3 etc.

c) Octal numbers, e.g. : -055 01234 0212

d) Positive octal numbers that begin with zero and negative octal numbers that start with −zero.

e) Hexadecimals e.g.: 0xFF , -0xCFFF. The positive hexadecimals begin with 0x and negative hexadecimals start with -0x .

f) Predefined mathematical constants, e.g. : Math.PI   //pi = 3.14159...

10. How can we test whether a particular variable holds a string or a number?

Answer: To test whether a variable holds a string or number is by using the *typeof* operator. In case the variable holds a string, *typeof(variable)* will return "string" and if it holds number than it will return "number".

In this chapter, we have covered the basic fundamentals of JavaScript which would have given you a fair idea on its working. By adding JavaScript to your HTML pages, you can make your website more dynamic and interactive. We also learned about some important concepts of this scripting language such as operators, functions, and variables and covered some standard programming concepts like if statements, switch statements and loops. However, it is a vast language and it offers loads of features and functions which can be learned and brought into practice with time.

How HTML5, CSS, and JavaScript work together?

HTML5 itself is a very powerful programming language but its actual power is realized when it is used with JavaScript and CSS3. JavaScript has undoubtedly emerged as one of the best scripting languages to render great visual effects to a website. Graphics libraries like WebGL in JavaScript allows developers to create interactive 3D graphics within the browser by utilizing the plugin free character of HTML canvas element.

All three languages are intertwined in the sense HTML provides the basic structure of web sites, which are enhanced and modified by JavaScript and CSS. CSS tells HTML what colors, fonts and other styles to be used and JavaScript tells HTML how to perform certain tasks like making a pop-up window etc.

The two most important things to keep in mind while learning web development are:

a) Use correct HTML tags – The structure of the content is described by different HTML tags and each tag has its own meaning and a defined place.

b) Keep your JavaScript, HTML and CSS code separate- Always put JavaScript and CSS in a separate file other than the HTML one. This will make your work simple and you will be able to manage better. So, by keeping all your styles and functional codes in one place will make things easy.

What's next?

It's easy to read through a book and think that you have got it and understand it but just reading a book once is simply not enough. Here are 5 tips to help you get the most out of your learning and go on to become, if not an expert, then at least proficient in JavaScript, CSS, and HTML.

1. Practice

And keep tracking your progress. If you have heard of the term, 'use it or lose it", it certainly applies to CSS, JavaScript, and HTML. Once you have learned the basics, you can't just walk away and expect it all to come back to you a month down the line. Nor can you expect things not to have changed. The nature of any programming language, low or high level is that it changes often and if you don't keep up with it, you will get left behind.

Constant practice will keep your brain ticking over and keep things fresh in your mind. There are plenty of websites that offer sample designs for you to try recreating and this is helpful because one of the things expected of a front-end developer is to be able to turn a design from a PSD into a code. There are also a couple of practical projects at the end of this book for you to keep practicing on as well.

As you keep on practicing, your skills will begin to sharpen up and you will start to learn new and better ways of doing something. Your work will become more streamlined and you will get faster. Eventually, you will be doing certain things without even thinking about them first. You might struggle to start with and you might think it's all a waste of time but you can't ignore it when things suddenly start to fall into place for you. Did you suddenly get faster at writing your body tags? Did you suddenly feel more comfortable about designing a web page? Then all that practice has paid off.

Don't forget to build up a portfolio of all your work as well. It doesn't matter if it's just a couple of pieces it's all testament to how you are progressing and, in years to come you will be able to look back and pinpoint where things started to go right for you.

2. Take Advanced Classes

You already learned the basics so go ahead and take some advanced classes in HTML CSS and JavaScript. Think about moving on to Sass, UX, and Responsive Web Design as well. There are plenty of advanced tutorials online, plenty of books and plenty of courses that you can sign up for. Once you are happy with the fundamentals move on, expand your knowledge and expand your learning.

3. Build a Resource List

No one class, video, book or course can possibly cover everything you need to know so start setting up a list of resources that you can go to when you need to know something specific. Go through the book listings on Amazon and pick the ones that are likely to help you the most. Look for podcasts, video tutorials and weekly or daily blog articles. Head to Udemy and find course that you can sign up for. Make sure you keep up to date with all the latest information and movements in all three languages otherwise you will get left behind.

4. Start Learning Design and UX (User Experience)

Many years ago, the late Steve Jobs was once heard to say, "Design is not just what it looks and feels like. Design is how it works." This is a mantra that you should repeat to yourself constantly until it is embedded in your brain. Whether you a designer or not, you do need to learn and understand the principles that underlie good design and UX. If you can learn UX and design you can move from building on and executing a vision that someone else had to create your own. Who doesn't want to be the one driving? Just to clear it up, UX is the art of designing something beautiful, simple, and easy to interact with, like a good website.

It doesn't matter whether this is where you see yourself heading in the future, it is good practice to have the skills, learn the language and understand the disciplines and principles – they are all useful skills to have, regardless of your role.

5. Leave Your Computer alone!

You don't need to do it all online, there is plenty of inspiration elsewhere. Look around your community, see if there any web design groups that meet up. See if there are any courses you can sign up to at your nearest technical college – learning online is one thing, getting together with other like-minded individuals is another ball game altogether. Not only will you learn more about HTML, CSS or JavaScript, you will also get to build up a community of people who can all learn off one another, people to bounce ideas off and learn new skills, tips, tricks, and shortcuts.

CHAPTER 10
JAVASCRIPT BEST PRACTICES

Before we move on to the practical side of things, these are some of the best practices you should learn with JavaScript:

Use === Instead of ==

There are two equality operators that javascript makes use of: === | ! == and == | !. Best practice dictates that you should use the use the first one when you are comparing. Generally, when you have two operands that are the same value and type, using === will produce true while ! == will produce False.

That said, when you use == and != you will come up against problems when you have different types; the operators will unsuccessfully attempt to coerce the values.

Eval = Bad

If you are not too familiar with this, the function called eval provides access to the compiler. If you pass a string as a parameter of eval, you can execute the result but this will result in the performance of the script decreasing substantially and it is a security risk. This is because it is giving way too much power to the text passed in so avoid using it!

Avoid Using Shorthand

Technically, you may get away with leaving out many of the semi colons and curly braces and many browsers will interpret this next code correctly:

```
if(aVariableExists)

  x = false
```

However, look at this one:

```
if(aVariableExists)

  x = false

  anotherFunctionCall();
```

You could be forgiven for thinking that this is the same as:

```
if(aVariableExists) {

  x = false;

  anotherFunctionCall();

}
```

But you would be wrong because, what it really means is:

```
if(aVariableExists) {

  x = false;

}
```

```
anotherFunctionCall();
```

As you can see, the indentation will mimic what the curly brace does but this is bad practice and you should avoid using it. There is only one instance where curly braces should be left out ad that is with one-liners – even that comes under heavy debate!

```
if(2 + 2 === 4) return 'well done';
```

Make use of JS Lint

JS Lint is one of the best debugger tools for JavaScript. All you need to do is paste your script in and JS Lint will scan it for any obvious errors or issues. If it finds anything, a message will be returned telling you what the problem is and approximately where in your script it is. It may be a syntax error, although most errors are, especially with beginners. Lint also looks at style and structure. JS Lint won't prove that your script is right, it just picks up on things that may well be missed otherwise. So, before you sign your script off, get into the habit of running it through JS Lint to make sure there aren't any silly mistakes

Scripts should be At the Bottom of the Page

I already mentioned this to you earlier but it is worth another mention. You want your page to load quickly and it can't if it has to wait until whole files have been uploaded first. Put your JavaScript files, particularly those that add some functionality, right at the bottom of the page to make things work properly. This is what it should be like:

```
<p>And now you know my favorite kinds of beans. </p>

<script type="text/javascript" src="path/to/file.js"></script>

<script type="text/javascript"
src="path/to/anotherFile.js"></script>

</body>

</html>
```

Variables Should Be Declared Outside the For Statement

When you have long For statements to execute, don't make things worse than they should be. For example, don't do this:

```
for(var i = 0; i < someArray.length; i++) {

  var container = document.getElementById('container');

  container.innerHtml += 'my number: ' + i;

  console.log(i);
```

```
}
```

Note that, for every iteration the array length has be determined and we are having to traverse dom to locate the container element every time. This is not efficient! This is how it should be done:

```
var container = document.getElementById('container');

for(var i = 0, len = someArray.length; i < len; i++) {

    container.innerHtml += 'my number: ' + i;

    console.log(i);

}
```

Build a String Quickly

You don't always need to use the for statement when you want to loop through an object or an array. Be a little creative and find a quicker way of doing it, something like this:

```
var arr = ['item 1', 'item 2', 'item 3', ...];

var list = '<ul><li>' + arr.join('</li><li>') + '</li></ul>';
```

One of the fastest ways is to use the join() method, a native JavaScript method, rather than attempting to use one that is not native, irrespective of what is happening underneath the abstraction layers.

Reduce Your Global Footprint

By keeping your global footprint down, you have a significant chance of reducing instances of bad interaction with other libraries, widgets or applications. Don't do it like this:

var name = 'Jonathon';

var lastName = 'White';

function doSomething() {...}

Do it like this:

console.log(name); // Jonathon -- or window.name

var DudeNameSpace = {

  name : 'Jonathon',

  lastName : 'White',

  doSomething : function() {...}

}

console.log(DudeNameSpace.name); // Jonathon

We have cut the footprint that the global used to just one object.

Use Comments All the Time

You might think it unnecessary but, believe me, comments are king in any computer programming language. When you come back to your code a few weeks later, you might forget what you were actually doing or what a specific part of the code was for. Adding comments all the time will help you and anyone else who needs to read or revise your code.

```
// Cycle through the array and then echo out each of the names.

for(var i = 0, len = array.length; i < len; i++) {

  console.log(array[i]);

}
```

Progressive Enhancement

You should always be thinking about the times when JavaScript may, for some reason, be disabled. You could get away with saying that most of your users will have it enabled but what about the handful that don't? - Those who won't be able to use your website? Forgetting about them is one of the biggest mistakes you can make.

Download the Web Developer Toolbar and view your site with JavaScript disabled. Look at all the wonderful things you designed and see just what happens when JavaScript isn't working. You should always design a website with the view that JavaScript is permanently disabled to that it will always work. That is progressive enhancement.

Never Pass Strings to "SetInterval" or "SetTimeOut"

Let me explain this with a bit of code:

setInterval(

"document.getElementById('container').innerHTML += 'My new number: ' + i", 3000

);

It doesn't look nice and it certainly isn't efficient Not only that, it works like the eval function works. Rather than passing a string, pass a function to SetInterval or SetTimeOut.

setInterval(someFunction, 3000);

Avoid the Use of the With Statement

When you first look at it, a with statement might seem like a good idea. The concept behind them is that you can use them as a shorthand way of getting to an object that is nested deeply. For example:

with (being.person.woman.bodyparts) {

  head = true;

  feet = true;

}

And not:

being.person.woman.bodyparts.head = true;

being.person.woman.bodyparts.feet= true;

Extensive testing showed that these don't behave very well when it comes to setting new members and that it is, in fact better to use var:

var o = being.person.wman.bodyparts;

o.head = true;

o.feet = true;

Don't Use New Object(); Use {}

There are loads of methods to creating new JavaScript objects and the more traditional way has always been to use the constructor called new, like this:

var o = new Object();

o.name = 'Jonathon';

o.lastName = 'White';

o.someFunction = function() {

  console.log(this.name);

```
}
```

However, although this technically isn't bad, it also isn't good practice. Instead, you should use the better object literal method, like this:

```
var o = {

  name: 'Jonathon',

  lastName = 'White',

  someFunction : function() {

    console.log(this.name);

  }

};
```

If you just wanted an empty object created, {} does the trick quite nicely:

```
var o = {};
```

An object literal lets you write code that has support for a ton of features but still enables that code to be straightforward enough for implementation. There really isn't any need to directly invoke a constructor not to maintain the right order of the arguments that are passed to the functions.

Don't Use New Array(); Use []

The same principle can be applied to the creation of a new array.

This is okay:

var a = new Array();

a[0] = "Ben";

a[1] = 'Electrician';

But this is better

var a = ['Ben','Electrician'];

One of the most common JavaScript errors is to use objects when arrays are needed and vice versa. It really is quite simple – if the property name is a sequential small integer, use the array; otherwise, objects should be used.

Leave Var Out and Use Commas for Long Variables Lists

Again, let me show you an example:

var anItem = 'a string';

var andAnotherItem = 'and another string';

var yetAnotherItem = 'yet another string';

This is much better:

```
var anItem = 'a string',

  andAnotherItem = 'and another string',

  yetAnotherItem = 'yet another string';
```

This should explain itself. You won't see any vast improvements in terms of speed here but your code will be cleaner

Use Semicolons!

Many browsers will allow you to omit the semicolon:

```
var anItem = 'a string'

function doSomething() {

  return 'something'

}
```

That said, , this is not good practice and it can lead on to worse issues that can't be found. A better way of doing it is:

```
var anItem = 'a string';

function doSomething() {

  return 'something';

}
```

Use For In Statements

When you are looping through object items, you may also be using retiree method functions. To get around this, wrap up your code in an if statement to filter out information:

```
for(key in object) {

  if(object.hasOwnProperty(key) {

    ...then do something...

  }

}
```

Use the Timer Feature on Firebug

If you want to know how long a specific operation will take, utilize the Timer feature on Firebug to keep a log of your results and optimize your code:

```
function TimeTracker(){

 console.time("MyTimer");

 for(x=5000; x > 0; x--){}

 console.timeEnd("MyTimer");

}
```

Read, Read, and Read Some More

Web development blogs are great for picking up information but there is no substitute for a proper book. Keep a stack of web development books by your bedside, one in your bag and ne by the sofa so you always have something to pick up and read and learn.

Use Self-Executing Functions

Instead of calling functions, it is very easy to get a function to automatically run when a parent function gets called or when a page loads, for example. All you do is wrap that function up inside a set of parentheses and then append an extra set – this will call the function.

```
(function doSomething() {

  return {

    name: jon,

    lastName: 'white'

  };
})();
```

Use Raw JavaScript Rather Than a Library – It's Quicker

JavaScript libraries, like Mootools and jQuery, can save lots of time when you are coding but it is worth bearing in mind that libraries are never going to be as quick as raw JavaScript is, always assuming that you are coding properly. For example, the 'each' method in jQuery is good for when you want to loop but it will always be that little bit quicker to use the 'for' statement, which is native.

Use a JSON Parser

Although it should be built-in to Javascript, if you are using a version that doesn't have on, you will need to implement a JSON parser. By importing this script, you can get into a new JSON global object and you can use that for parsing your own .json file:

```
var response = JSON.parse(xhr.responseText);

var container = document.getElementById('container');

for(var i = 0, len = response.length; i < len; i++) {

  container.innerHTML += '<li>' + response[i].name + ' : ' + response[i].email + '</li>';

}
```

Remove the Language Attribute

Many years back, it would be common to find a language attriute inside the script tags:

<script type="text/javascript" language="javascript">

...

</script>

These days there is no need to use it and it has now been deprecated so get into the habit of not using it

CHAPTER 11
PRACTICAL PROJECTS

Template for a One-Page CSS3 and HTML Website

Code courtesy of www.tutorialzine.com

For this project, we are going to look at building a template for an HTML5 website and we will be using some of the better features in CSS3 and jQuery, including a scrollTo plugin.

The Design

When you start your design, you always begin with an idea, one that you can build on as you go along or at a later date. At this stage, many designers tend to start with a program like Photoshop, just to see what it would all look like and to work out the details. Once you have done that you then code the design using HTML5 and CSS, starting with the design of the background, the fonts and the colors and then moving on to content section.

HTML

Right now, although it has been out for a couple of years, work on HTML5 is still ongoing and, in all honesty, it probably will be for the next 5 years or so. However, some of it is ready for use now. What we are going to use with this template are some of the tags that HTML5 introduced:

- <header> - to wrap your page header in

- <footer> - to wrap your page footer in

- <section> - to group your content into different sections, such as sidebar, main area, etc.

- <article> - to separate individual articles from the remainder of the page

- <nav> - where your navigation menu goes

- <figure> - can contain an image that you are using in your article

We will use these in the same way that we use divs with the only real difference being that these tags will organize your page in a better way. In other words, your content can be presented in a way that the content can be better determined by the search engines and, as a result, you should get more visitors and hopefully, more revenue, depending on what your site is all about of course.

That said, there are one or two implications with HTML5, one of them being the Internet Explorer browsers. These browsers do not support the HTML tags but we can get around that easily using a simple JavaScript file. Ready? We are going to use a template supplied by www.tutorialzine.com just to give you an idea of what you can do and how it all works. Either type this, exactly, or copy and paste it into your text editor.

template.html - Head section

<!DOCTYPE html> <!-- The new doctype -->

<html>

<head>

  <meta http-equiv="Content-Type" content="text/html; charset=utf-8" />

  <title>Coding A CSS3 & HTML5 One Page Template | Tutorialzine demo</title>

  <link rel="stylesheet" type="text/css" href="styles.css" />

  <!-- Internet Explorer HTML5 enabling script: -->

  <!--[if IE]>

    <script src="http://html5shiv.googlecode.com/svn/trunk/html5.js"></script>

    <style type="text/css">

```
      .clear {

         zoom: 1;

         display: block;

      }

   </style>

 <![endif]-->

</head>
```

Note the new <DOCTYPE> on the first line. This is telling your browser that you have used HTML5 standard for creating the page with. And, if you are used to using HTML4, you will notice that it is shorter and much easier than the old doctypes to remember.

After we have specified the document and title encoding, we need to add in a special JavaScript file that will let any version of Internet Explorer render the HTML5 tags correctly. That way, if a visitor comes to your site via Internet Explorer, and they have JavaScript enabled, it will render fine. However, if they have disabled JavaScript, all they will see is a mess.

Copy and paste or type this to the bottom of your code in the text editor

template.html - Body Section

```html
<body>

  <section id="page"> <!-- Define the #page section using the
  section tag -->

  <header> <!-- Define the header section of the page using the
  appropriate tag -->

    <h1>Your Site Logo</h1>

    <h3>and a nice slogan</h3>

    <nav class="clear"> <!-- The nav link will mark your main
    site navigation semantically -->

      <ul>

        <li><a href="#article1">Photoshoot</a></li>

        <li><a href="#article2">Sweet Tabs</a></li>

        <li><a href="#article3">Navigation Menu</a></li>

      </ul>

    </nav>

  </header>
```

Note that we have used the new HTML5 section tags to divide the page into different sections. The outermost tag is the #page section and we have set that to a standard 960px in the style sheet. This will enable older computers to display the site properly.

This is followed by the header and navigation tags. Note that we have given the links an href attribute – the bit that follows the # corresponds to the article ID that we are scrolling to.

template.html - Article

```
<!-- Article 1 start -->

<div class="line"></div>  <!-- Dividing line -->

<article id="article1"> <!-- The new article tag. We supply the
id so that it will easily scroll into view. -->

  <h2>Photoshoot Effect</h2>

  <div class="line"></div>

  <div class="articleBody clear">

    <figure> <!-- The figure tag marks the data, usually an
image, that is included in the article -->

      <a        href="https://tutorialzine.com/2010/02/photo-
shoot-css-jquery/">

        <img
src="https://tutorialzine.com/img/featured/641.jpg"
width="620" height="340" /></a>
```

```
</figure>

<p>
```

What we are doing here is making an effect like a photo shoot using the PhotoShoot jQuery plugin. You can use this to turn a normal <div> on your page to a photo-shoot stage that has a feel to it like it is a camera shoot.

```
</p>

        <p>Lorem ipsum dolor sit amet, consectetur adipiscing
```
elit. Integer luctus quam quis .... </p>

```
    </div>

    </article>

    <!-- Article 1 end -->
```

We have shared this markup with all the articles. The dividing line comes first – ideally, the best way to do this is to use an <hr> line and in HTML5 this is used as a logical dividing element. Sadly, it isn't possible to do this for a site we are styling for all browsers so you need to stick to using the <div>.

This is followed by the article tag, using a unique id which navigation will then use for scrolling the page. The article title is inside together with a couple of paragraphs and figure tags, marking the fact that we have images in the article.

template.html - Footer

```
<footer> <!-- Marks the footer section -->

    <div class="line"></div>

    <p>Copyright 2010 - YourSite.com</p> <!-- Change the
copyright notice -->

    <a href="#" class="up">Go UP</a>

    <a href="https://tutorialzine.com/" class="by">Template
by Tutorialzine</a>

</footer>

</section> <!-- Close the #page section -->

<!-- JavaScript Includes -->

<script
src="http://ajax.googleapis.com/ajax/libs/jquery/1.3.2/jquery.mi
n.js"></script>

<script            src="jquery.scrollTo-1.4.2/jquery.scrollTo-
min.js"></script>

<script src="script.js"></script>

</body>

</html>
```

Finally, we have a footer tag and this does what its meant to do. At the very bottom, we have all the JavaScript includes, adding the scrollTo plugin and the jQuery library.

CSS

Because we have used HTML5, there are some extra things to do when it comes to styling. The new HTML5 tags don't yet have a default styling attached to them so we need to add some CSS code in to make everything look and work as it should do.

styles.css - Part 1

```
header,footer,

article,section,

hgroup,nav,

figure{

    /* Providing a display value to the HTML5 rendered elements:
*/

    display:block;

}

article .line{

    /* The dividing line inside the article is darker: */
```

```css
    background-color:#15242a;

    border-bottom-color:#204656;

    margin:1.3em 0;
}
footer .line{

    margin:2em 0;
}
nav{

    background:url(img/gradient_light.jpg)  repeat-x  50%  50%
#f8f8f8;

    padding:0 5px;

    position:absolute;

    right:0;

    top:4em;

    border:1px solid #FCFCFC;

    -moz-box-shadow:0 1px 1px #333333;

    -webkit-box-shadow:0 1px 1px #333333;

    box-shadow:0 1px 1px #333333;
```

```css
}

nav ul li{

    display:inline;

}

nav ul li a,

nav ul li a:visited{

    color:#565656;

    display:block;

    float:left;

    font-size:1.25em;

    font-weight:bold;

    margin:5px 2px;

    padding:7px 10px 4px;

    text-shadow:0 1px 1px white;

    text-transform:uppercase;

}

nav ul li a:hover{
```

```css
    text-decoration:none;

    background-color:#f0f0f0;

}

nav, article, nav ul li a,figure{

    /* Applying CSS3 rounded corners: */

    -moz-border-radius:10px;

    -webkit-border-radius:10px;

    border-radius:10px;

}
```

That I quite a lot of code but what we have done here is blocked by setting the display value for the tags. Then we can style them in the same way that we do with normal divs. The horizontal line, navigation buttons and articles are all styled, with the nav buttons being listed inside the nav tag as an unordered list. Lastly, the border-radius properties are supplied for 4 different elements at once, thus saving a whole lot of typing extra code.

styles.css - Part 2

```css
/* Article styles: */

#page{
```

```css
    width:960px;

    margin:0 auto;

    position:relative;
}
article{

    background-color:#213E4A;

    margin:3em 0;

    padding:20px;

    text-shadow:0 2px 0 black;
}
figure{

    border:3px solid #142830;

    float:right;

    height:300px;

    margin-left:15px;

    overflow:hidden;

    width:500px;
```

```css
}

figure:hover{

    -moz-box-shadow:0 0 2px #4D7788;

    -webkit-box-shadow:0 0 2px #4D7788;

    box-shadow:0 0 2px #4D7788;

}

figure img{

    margin-left:-60px;

}

/* Footer styling: */

footer{

    margin-bottom:30px;

    text-align:center;

    font-size:0.825em;

}

footer p{

    margin-bottom:-2.5em;
```

```css
    position:relative;

}

footer a,footer a:visited{

    color:#cccccc;

    background-color:#213e4a;

    display:block;

    padding:2px 4px;

    z-index:100;

    position:relative;

}

footer a:hover{

    text-decoration:none;

    background-color:#142830;

}

footer a.by{

    float:left;

}
```

```
footer a.up{

   float:right;

}
```

In this next bit of code, we have given more detail to the styling of the elements, including giving the page section some width providing the figure tag with a hover property and providing the links in the footer with some styling.

jQuery

To give the template a better look, we are going to give it a nice smooth scrolling effect as soon as a navigation link gets clicked and this is done with the jQuery scrollTo plugin that we put in earlier. For it to work though, we must loop through all the links included in the nav bar not forgetting the UP link that is in the page footer and then assign it an onclick event. This will trigger the function defined by that plugin.

script.js

```
$(document).ready(function(){

   /* This code is executed after the DOM has been completely
loaded */

   $('nav a,footer a.up').click(function(e){
```

```
    // If a link has been clicked, scroll the page to the link's hash
target:

    $.scrollTo( this.hash || 0, 1500);

    e.preventDefault();

  });

});
```

And that is your template complete. The thing to do now is to play around with, change elements, add things in and see what you can do with it. This is only a template so the world is your oyster.

HTML5 and CSS3 Website

This is another website built using HTML5 and CSS 3 and we are going to do it in 2 parts. First, we build the outline using HTML5 and then we use CSS3 to format it and lay out the page.

The code in this section has been provided courtesy of www.openclassrooms.com

HTML

The first thing we need to do is work out the main blocks which are going to form the outline of your page. We are going to use several different HTML tags, including the structural tags, like <header>, <footer>, etc. and the all-purpose <div> tag.

It is up to you to determine which tags you want to use but do make sure that you use tags that make sense. If there isn't one that fits what you want to do, use the <div> tag, which is generic.

The HTML5 code is the easiest part of building a website and, if you understand how tag nesting works, you should be able to run up a piece of code that is similar to this without any trouble.

```
<!DOCTYPE html>

<html>

  <head>

    <meta charset="utf-8" />

    <link rel="stylesheet" href="style.css" />

    <title>Gaby - Travel diaries</title>

  </head>

  <body>

    <div id="main_wrapper">

      <header>

        <div id="main_title">

          <img src="images/Gaby_logo.png" alt="Logo de Gaby" id="logo" />
```

```html
    <h1>Gaby</h1>

    <h2>Travel diaries</h2>

  </div>

  <nav>

    <ul>

      <li><a href="#">Home</a></li>

      <li><a href="#">Blog</a></li>

      <li><a href="#">Resume</a></li>

      <li><a href="#">Contact</a></li>

    </ul>

  </nav>

</header>

<div id="banner_image">

  <div id="banner_description">

    Reflections on a great vacation in Canada...

    <a href="#" class="red_button">See article <img src="images/small_arrow.png" alt="" /></a>

  </div>
```

```html
    </div>

    <section>

        <article>

            <h1><img src="images/pin.png" alt="Travel category" class="ico_categorie" />I'm a great traveler</h1>

            <p>Lorem ipsum dolor sit amet...</p>

            <p>Vivamus sed libero nec mauris pulvinar facilisis ut non sem...</p>

            <p>Phasellus ligula massa, congue ac vulputate non, dignissim at augue...</p>

        </article>

        <aside>

            <h1>About the author</h1>

            <img src="images/arrow.png.png" alt="" id="arrow" />

            <p id="Gaby_picture"><img src="images/images/Gaby.png" alt="Gaby Picture" /></p>

            <p>Allow me to introduce myself: My name's Gaby. I was born on 22 November 2000.</p>
```

```html
    <p>Not a lot there, is there? That's why I've decided to
write a biography to tell my readers know who I am.</p>

    <p><img src="images/facebook.png" alt="Facebook"
/><img src="images/twitter.png" alt="Twitter" /><img
src="images/vimeo.png" alt="Vimeo" /><img
src="images/flickr.png" alt="Flickr" /><img
src="images/rss.png" alt="RSS" /></p>

    </aside>

  </section>

  <footer>

    <div id="tweet">

      <h1>My last tweet</h1>

      <p>Ha-Ha!</p>

      <p>12/05 23:12</p>

    </div>

    <div id="my_pictures">

      <h1>My pictures</h1>

      <p><img src="images/pic1.jpg" alt="Picture" /><img
src="images/pic2.jpg" alt="Picture" /><img
```

```
src="images/pic3.jpg" alt="Picture" /><img
src="images/pic4.jpg" alt="Picture" /></p>

        </div>

        <div id="my_friends">

          <h1>My friends</h1>

          <ul>

            <li><a href="#">Pipi the rabbit</a></li>

            <li><a href="#">Mr Bab</a></li>

            <li><a href="#">Kaiwaii</a></li>

            <li><a href="#">Percival.eu</a></li>

          </ul>

          <ul>

            <li><a href="#">Ji</a></li>

            <li><a href="#">Super tomato</a></li>

            <li><a href="#">Princess</a></li>

            <li><a href="#">Mr Fang</a></li>

          </ul>

        </div>
```

```
        </footer>

      </div>

    </body>

  </html>
```

Small note here. Notice that we put the entire contents of the page inside a bit <div> tag using a main_wrapper if. Because this one tag has all the content, it will be much easier to work out the size of the page and to get the website centered on the screen.

Besides that, it is all quite straightforward. I havent particularly added all the tags in straightway; when you get to designing it in CSS, you will probably need to include some tags in a <div> block to help you get things right.

So, the page doesn't look that fantastic yet but the best is yet to come because the CSS will provide all the magic we need!

CSS

This is where things get a bit tougher. It will take work to get a result that you want although, at this stage, don't be seeing perfection because you won't find it. If your website looks great in one browser, you can be sure that in another one there will be a problem or two. There may even be differences when the website is displayed on a computer screen that is different to the one you are using. Just do your best and even that is going to take some work!

We will do the next bit, all the formatting and designing in a few steps, in this order:

- Customizing the font

- Defining the main style – width, color of the background, what default color the text will be

- Header and the browsing links

- A banner – this one will have San Francisco bridge on it

- The main part of the body

- The footer

Customizing the Font

We will use three fonts here but I urge you to use the ones you are comfortable with, especially as the second two need to be downloaded from the internet. Please just use this as a template and pick two fonts that will look nice:

- Trebuchet MS

- Ballpark Weiner

- Day Roman

You will already have Trebuchet on your computer but the others are a little on the special side and may not be on the computers of your visitors. As is said, pick two others that are on your computer and use those in place.

```css
/* Define the custom fonts */

@font-face

{

    font-family: 'BallparkWeiner';

    src: url('fonts/ballpark.eot');

    src: url('fonts/ballpark.eot?#iefix') format('embedded-opentype'),

        url('fonts/ballpark.woff') format('woff'),

        url('fonts/ballpark.ttf') format('truetype'),

        url('fonts/ballpark.svg#BallparkWeiner') format('svg');

    font-weight: normal;

    font-style: normal;

}

@font-face

{
```

```css
    font-family: 'Dayrom';

    src: url('fonts/dayrom.eot');

    src: url('fonts/dayrom.eot?#iefix') format('embedded-
opentype'),

        url('fonts/dayrom.woff') format('woff'),

        url('fonts/dayrom.ttf') format('truetype'),

        url('fonts/dayrom.svg#Dayrom') format('svg');

    font-weight: normal;

    font-style: normal;

}
```

As well as this, the fonts you are using must be made available – I have provided a font subfolder for all the different versions of the fonts used.

The Main Styles

Now we need to add some global styles for the page design. We will define a background image, the font and the color of the text and, more importantly, we will size the page and have it centered on screen

```css
/* Main elements of the page */
```

```css
body
{
    background: url('images/yellow_background.png');
    font-family: 'Trebuchet MS', Arial, sans-serif;
    color: #181818;
}
#main_wrapper
{
    width: 900px;
    margin: auto;
}
section h1, footer h1, nav a
{
    font-family: Dayrom, serif;
    font-weight: normal;
    text-transform: uppercase;
}
```

By using #bloc page, the block will cover the whole pages we set the width to a limit of 900 px and, with automatic margins, the design gets centered. If you wanted your design to fit the screens of your visitors, you would set the width in percentage rather than pixels.

There is a new one here – the CSS propertytext-transform: uppercase. This makes sure that titles are always in uppercase, changing them where needed.

Header and Browsing Links

You don't have to include browsing links in your header if you don't want to but this shows you how to do it if you want to. The first thing to do is define the header, especially the logo and then we will look at formatting the browsing links:

The header
/* Header */

header

{

    background: url('images/line.png') repeat-x bottom;

}

#main_title

{

```css
    display: inline-block;

}

header h1

{

    font-family: 'BallparkWeiner', serif;

    font-size: 2.5em;

    font-weight: normal;

}

#logo, header h1

{

    display: inline-block;

    margin-bottom: 0px;

}

header h2

{

    font-family: Dayrom, serif;

    font-size: 1.1em;
```

```
    margin-top: 0px;

    font-weight: normal;

}
```

We are going to use a background image to distinguish between the header and the body of the page. We use inline-block to position the items and then customize the fonts and the sizes. This is nothing too difficult for now.

When it comes to the browsing links, the formatting starts to get a bit more interesting. We have a bullet-point list of the links but these are generally not displayed width-wise; they are usually height-wise. That is easy to change:

```
/* Navigation */

nav

{

    display: inline-block;

    width: 740px;

    text-align: right;

}

nav ul
```

```css
{
    list-style-type: none;
}
nav li
{
    display: inline-block;
    margin-right: 15px;
}
nav a
{
    font-size: 1.3em;
    color: #181818;
    padding-bottom: 3px;
    text-decoration: none;
}
nav a:hover
{
```

```
    color: #760001;

    border-bottom: 3px solid #760001;

}
```

One of the biggest new things to hit CSS3 is the definition list-style-type: none; which is responsible for moving the bullet, which is a round image. Each of the list items, <li> holds a position as an online-block and this lets us put the links beside one another, instead of one on top of the other.

The rest of the definitions are nothing special – simply colors, dimensions, borders, etc., all things you should already know about. You may not get the right values in the first time around; it is trial and error, like everything else, to get the appearance that you want.

The Banner

Next, we turn to the banner, something a little more interesting but more difficult nonetheless. The banner has several points of interest:

- The edges are rounded

- The background upon which the description is written is a little transparent

- We implemented the "see the article" button in CSS using rounded edges

- We use a shadow to give the banner a little volume

Here's how to produce a banner with a picture of the San Francisco bridge on it. To change the picture to something else, simply import another picture:

```
/* Banner */

#banner_image

{

    margin-top: 15px;

    height: 200px;

    border-radius: 5px;

    background: url('images/sanfrancisco.jpg') no-repeat;

    position: relative;

    box-shadow: 0px 4px 4px #1c1a19;

    margin-bottom: 25px;

}

#banner_description
```

```
{

    position: absolute;

    bottom: 0;

    border-radius: 0px 0px 5px 5px;

    width: 99.5%;

    height: 33px;

    padding-top: 15px;

    padding-left: 4px;

    background-color: rgb(24,24,24); /* Older browsers can read
this */

    background-color: rgba(24,24,24,0.8); /* Newer browsers can
read this */

    color: white;

    font-size: 0.8em;

}

.red_button

{

    display: inline-block;
```

```
    height: 25px;

    position: absolute;

    right: 5px;

    bottom: 5px;

    background: url('images/red_background.png') repeat-x;

    border: 1px solid #760001;

    border-radius: 5px;

    font-size: 1.2em;

    text-align: center;

    padding: 3px 8px 0px 8px;

    color: white;

    text-decoration: none;
}
.red_button img
{
    border: 0;
}
```

This is somewhat technical and is packed with CSS features – it is most likely the most difficult bit of the whole website.

Note that the bridge is displayed as a background using the banner<div> block. It has also been given a position that is relative to it without needing to use any properties to change the offset. Why did we do this? A relative position with no offset normally has no purpose but, in this case, it was useful when it came to putting the "See Article" button under the banner on the right. The button has been placed inside in an absolute position. So, why is it there? Why not at the bottom of the page?

No. Remember, if blocks are placed in absolute positions in other blocks, which is also an absolute, relative or fixed position, it then gets positioned within that block. Because the banner has a relative position with no offset, and the button has an absolute position inside, it gets placed under the banner at the bottom right corner.

Remember this technique – it is powerful and it can be incredibly helpful when building your design.

Lastly, for the banner, we have used transparency with the RGB annotation and not with the opacity property. If we had used the latter, the contents of the whole block would have been transparent and that includes the "see article" button. It is better to just have the background transparent.

The "see article" button has graduated color on it and to do this we used an image for the background that represents the graduation and this has been represented in a horizontal manner. You may use a CSS3 linear-gradient property to produce these graduations without needing to use a background image. However, that is somewhat more complex than we need to go into right now so we will stick with the easier way of using the image.

The Body

The body of the page is in the center and, in our case, it has one <section> tag – you could have used several tags if you wanted. The body is somewhat easier. We position the "About the author" block as an inline-block. We are going to play around with the shadows and the corners and then change the size and the text margins.

```
/* Body */

article, aside

{

    display: inline-block;

    vertical-align: top;

    text-align: justify;

}
```

```css
article
{
    width: 625px;
    margin-right: 15px;
}
.cat_icon
{
    vertical-align: middle;
    margin-right: 8px;
}
article p
{
    font-size: 0.8em;
}
aside
{
    position: relative;
```

```css
    width: 235px;

    background-color: #706b64;

    box-shadow: 0px 2px 5px #1c1a19;

    border-radius: 5px;

    padding: 10px;

    color: white;

    font-size: 0.9em;
}
#arrow
{

    position: absolute;

    top: 100px;

    left: -12px;
}
#Gaby_picture
{

    text-align: center;
```

```
}

#Gaby_picture img

{

   border: 1px solid #181818;

}

aside img

{

   margin-right: 5px;

}
```

The hardest part here is in putting the arrow to the left side of the "About the author" block, producing a bubble effect. Again, absolute positioning comes into play and we use the same technique. The <aside> block is positioned relatively with no offset and that lets us put the image of the arrow relative to that block and not to the entire page. By making an adjustment to the offset it can be placed exactly where you want it.

The Footer

What's left to do is the footer, which has three sub-blocks in it. These are produced using <div> with an id assigned to help better identify them. We then position the blocks in side line-block, beside one another.

```
/* Footer */

footer

{

    background:    url('images/top.png')  no-repeat  top  center,
url('images/line.png')  repeat-x  top,  url('images/shadow.png')
repeat-x top;

    padding-top: 25px;

}

footer p, footer ul

{

    font-size: 0.8em;

}

footer h1

{

    font-size: 1.1em;

}
```

```
#tweet, #my_pictures, #my_friends

{

    display: inline-block;

    vertical-align: top;

}

#tweet

{

    width: 28%;

}

#my_pictures

{

    width: 35%;

}

#my_friends

{

    width: 31%;

}
```

```css
#my_pictures img

{

   border: 1px solid #181818;

   margin-right: 2px;

}

#my_friends ul

{

   display: inline-block;

   vertical-align: top;

   margin-top: 0;

   width: 48%;

   list-style-image: url('images/external_link.png');

   padding-left: 2px;

}

#my_friends a

{

   text-decoration: none;
```

```
  color: #760001;

}
```

A couple of things to note about the footer. We used the multiple background images function in CSS3 to keep the footer and the body separate. There are three images in it – the separator, an upward arrow and a small graduation.

The bullet points for the "My Friends" list, located bottom-right, has been changed with the use of the list-style-image property and this lets us make use of a custom image instead of sticking with the standard bullet points. You will find, as you go along, that there are loads of CSS properties like this and you will have some fun learning how they all work.

That is the design completed but we are not finished yet! The design is one thing but now we need to test out this website on different browsers. In an ideal world, you would do this at every stage of the design, especially when it comes to the older Internet Explorer versions, which some people are still running, as the result might not be quite what you expect.

Internet Explorer Compatibility

Since Internet Explorer 9 was released a few years ago, there is no longer any of the famous lag that we used to see with Internet Explorer and CSS. However, the older versions need some work.

To see what your results would be in Internet Explorer 6 through 8, you can do one of two things:

- Use IE Tester, a tool that isn't very stable but is practical and, provided it doesn't crash it will show you what your website will look like

- Press the F12 key on your keyboard when you are using Internet Explorer 9 or above and a bar will appear. This is a web developer bar and it has a menu that lets you change the behavior for Internet Explorer so that you can simulate the older versions.

How to Change the Internet Explorer Rendering Engine

If you saw how your website looked on an older version of Internet Explorer, you would probably tear all your hair out and run away! But, there is no need to panic because there is always a solution. The website we are building will run into just two problems in older IE versions:

- Internet Explorer 6 and 7 do not handle inline-block positioning very well and the result will be that most of the tags for positioning won't work

- HTML5 tags for structuring are also not handled very well in Internet Explorer 6 through 8 and this can cause some very serious issues in the display. You can add a small script to the start of your code though, more about that in a minute.

What you will have to do is forget about using some of the newer CSS3 features that won't work in older IE versions, such as:

- Nice round corners

- Use of multiple images on the background

- Transparency

- Shadows

These are all features related to appearance and it isn't always worth getting them working in older versions of the browser. Again, there is a script you can use to emulate many of these features but this take a lot of work and is a bit more advanced than this tutorial will allow for. Not only that, your website could end up being painfully slow in the older browsers. As the vast majority of users will be on newer versions or on other browsers altogether, so long as you can get your website readable and looking good in those, I wouldn't worry too much.

HTML5 Structural Tags

As I said, we can add in a small JavaScript code to your website header and this will be sufficient:

<!DOCTYPE html>

<html>

  <head>

```
<meta charset="utf-8" />

<link rel="stylesheet" href="style.css" />

<!--[if lt IE 9]>

<script
src="http://html5shiv.googlecode.com/svn/trunk/html5.js"></s
cript>

<![endif]-->

<title>Gaby - Travel diaries</title>

</head>
```

We will download the required JavaScript file using the Google servers; it is much quicker and we won't need to manage the file ourselves.

Adjustment of the Inline-Block Position

To manage this, we can use a style sheet created especially for the older Internet Explorer versions. We need to use a slightly different CSS to make sure that the older browsers now what to do. By producing and using the special style sheet, and then using the following technique, you can come up with a reproduction of the way inline-block tags work.

```
<!DOCTYPE html>
```

```
<html>

  <head>

    <meta charset="utf-8" />

    <link rel="stylesheet" href="style.css" />

    <!--[if lte IE 7]>

    <link rel="stylesheet" href="style_ie.css" />

    <![endif]-->

    <title>Gaby - The Web Site</title>

  </head>
```

Thestyle_ie.cssstylesheet will contain statements like this:

```
element

{

  display: inline;

  zoom: 1;

}
```

You will need to apply this technique to each of the items that you positioned with the inline-block.

Validity Checking

W3C is one of the companies responsible for the standardization of HTML and they provide a validation tool called the Validator. This is a program that will analyze all your source code and it will let you know if you have written it properly or if there are any errors that need fixing.

There are two validators – one for HTML5 and one for CSS. The latter may still be a little buggy but nothing that impacts too much. The HTML validator, on the other hand, is incredibly useful. There are three tabs to the tool, allowing you three different ways to validate your web site:

- By the URL or address

- By sending the .html file

- By pasting the HTML code

Obviously, for the first one, you will need a domain name and URL so it's best to start by sending the file or pasting the code into the tool. If you send your code file and it all checks out, you will get a message that reads, "This document was successfully checked as HTML5!" There are no errors and you are good to go. This, however, is rare and you will more likely get an error message. No need to panic though; although your website may have looked nice, you still get the error message. Understand this – just because a website looks nice, it doesn't mean it isn't riddled with errors – you simply cannot equate one with the other. Browsers make every effort not to show the errors when they find them so they don't upset the user. There is, however, nothing to say that another browser won't make things look strange. Having a web page that is valid lets you rest a little easier, knowing that everything has been done right. This makes it easier for those programs that read the pages on each website and, a website that has been built properly is far more likely to have a good ranking in the search engines than one that hasn't – and that is a proven fact.

These tips can help you in your troubleshooting when errors are reported, as they will be at one time or another:

- All texts should be inside paragraph tags. You cannot put text between body tags without those tags being surrounded by paragraph tags. The same applies to <br /> line returns that must also be inside paragraphs. This is common with beginners.

<p>The text is placed correctly in a paragraph.

Don't forget that
 tags must also be inside a paragraph</p>

The text is incorrectly placed outside a paragraph. This is not allowed.

`<br />`

- Every image needs an alt attribute that specifies what is in the image. If your image, by any small chance, is just for decoration and you can't locate a description for it, you may put the value of the alt attribute down as nothing.

`<!-- The image has a description -->`

`<img src="picture.jpg" alt="My picture" />`

`<!-- The image doesn't have a description but it still has an alt attribute -->`

`<img src="deco.png" alt="" />`

The tags need to be closed in the correct order.

`<!-- These tags have not been closed in the order in which they were opened -->`

`<p>Important <em>text</p></em>`

`<!-- These tags have been closed in the order in which they were opened-->`

`<p>Important <em>text</em></p>`

This is a common mistake for beginners so keep the above scheme firm in your mind

- If you have & in your links, they must be replaced with the & code so that browser confusion is avoided.

<!—This is an example of an incorrect HTML link -->

<a href="http://www.site.com/?day=15&month=10&year=2000">

<!—This is an example of a correct HTML link -->

<a href="http://www.site.com/?day=15&month=10&year =2000">

- Lastly, ensure that have only used current tags and not the old or obsolete ones in HTML5.

We all make mistakes; no-one is infallible. There is no need to panic. Simply make the corrections, one step at a time until the validator tells you that you have an error-free website.

CONCLUSION

We have now come to the end of this book on web programming with HTML, CSS and JavaScript. All of these programming languages are quite vast in their own right. However, since they are simple and easy, you should not have too much of a problem in mastering them. With hard work and a bit of time, you will be able to create full-fledged websites in no time at all.

Of course, this book should have given you enough to have a good base on all three languages. You should have already seen the hello world examples and noted how easy they are. As such, you should have no problems with the basic syntax for each language.

You will have come across the basic functions, statements, and tags that are commonly used in these languages. More importantly, you should no longer have any problems in using them in a web page of your creation.

In HTML, you came to know how a simple web page can be written and filled with content. Then, with CSS, you will have been able to stylize that web page and make it look attractive. Finally, JavaScript allowed you to make your web page more interactive. As such, your web page should now be looking feeling a lot like the web pages you have previously admired over the internet.

With the end of this book, I wish you all the best for your future in programming. It is an exciting activity and one that will be useful for your career in the long run.

Thank you

Thank you very much for taking your time and reading through the book. I hope this book had tremendous value for you and helped you to master the basics of HTML.

Out of all the HTML related books you chose this book.

Thank you very much again for giving it a chance. It's now time to take what you just learned into action!

At this part, I'd like to ask you for a 'little' favor. May it be possible to leave a review for this guide on Amazon?

1 star – I really didn't like it

2 stars – it was okay

3 stars – I enjoyed it but it wasn't the best

4 stars – I really enjoyed it

5 stars – I LOVED it

Your review and feedback means a lot to us. Based on your feedback we can evaluate what you liked and what we can improve. Let us know how we can help you becoming a master programmer. On behalf of Joseph Connor, we from MJGPublishing are deeply grateful.

Last but not least, receive the latest information on programming by subscribing to our newsletter:
https://www.itstarterseries.com/newsletter

Contact us at MJGPublishing at any time:
marco@mjgpublishing.com

Bibliography

CodesCracker. (n.d.). *CSS Selectors*. Retrieved February 18, 2017, from CodesCracker: http://codescracker.com/css/css-selectors.htm

Hadlock, K. (2011, April 05). *Get Started with the JavaScript language, Part 1: JavaScript language fundamentals*. Retrieved February 18, 2017, from IBM developerWorks: https://www.ibm.com/developerworks/library/wa-javascriptstart/

Riwalk. (2010, July 27). *The Internet Explorer Z-Index Bug*. Retrieved February 18, 2017, from Coffeine on Code: http://caffeineoncode.com/2010/07/the-internet-explorer-z-index-bug/

Shabeena. (2016, March 30). *What are some uses of Javascript?* Retrieved February 18, 2017, from Quora: https://www.quora.com/What-are-some-uses-of-JavaScript

Tutorial Republic. (n.d.). *CSS Position*. Retrieved February 18, 2017, from Tutorial Republic: http://www.tutorialrepublic.com/css-tutorial/css-position.php

Tutorials Point. (n.d.). *HTML Lists*. Retrieved February 18, 2017, from Tutorials Point:

https://www.tutorialspoint.com/html/html_lists.htm

Open Classrooms (2017, June 12) Build Your Website with HTML5 and CSS3. Retrieved July 27, 2017 from Open Clasrooms

https://openclassrooms.com

TutorialZine (2010, February 16) Coding a CSS3 and HTML5 One-Page Website. Retrieved Jluy 27, 2017 from TutorialZine

https://tutorialzine.com

Free Video Course: Introduction to JavaScript, SQL & C++

I really hope that you enjoyed the book! You are now familiar with the first steps on Computer Programming. It's now time to take action!

Click the below image or link to get immediate access:

Click this link: **http://www.itstarterseries.com/free-programming-course** **NOW** and get immediate access to your free video series!

Happy coding,
Marco

Want to Learn more about Programming?

Check out the other books by Joseph Connor:

<u>Newest release (2017):</u> **Programming: Computer Programming For Beginners: Learn the Basics of SQL**

C#: Computer Programming for Beginners: Learn the Basics of C Sharp Programming – 3rd Edition (2017)

Python: The Definitive Guide to Learning Python Programming for Beginners

Hacking: Hacking for Beginners - Computer Virus, Cracking, Malware, IT Security

The Amazon Bestseller: Programming: Computer Programming for Beginners: Learn the Basics of Java, SQL & C++ - 4. Edition (2017)

CPSIA information can be obtained
at www.ICGtesting.com
Printed in the USA
LVOW03s2148230917
549823LV00003B/937/P